Mathematics through the senses, games, da

Z. P. Dienes

Director, Centre de Recherches en Psycho-Mathematique
University of Sherbrooke, Quebec, Canada

NFER Publishing Company Ltd.

Published by The NFER Publishing Company Ltd.
Book Division: 2 Jennings Buildings, Thames Ave.,
Windsor, Berks. SL1 2DQ.
Registered Office: The Mere, Upton Park,
Slough, Bucks. SL4 1QS.

First published 1973
© Z. P. Dienes, 1973
SBN 901225 87 8

Printed in Great Britain by
Direct Design (Bournemouth) Ltd.

Cover design by Amanda Prout

Distributed in The USA by
Fernhill House, Humanities Press Inc.,
450 Park Avenue South, New York, NY10016, USA.

KMM
7-16-84

Contents

Introduction

THIS IS WRITTEN in the hope of encouraging the beginnings of co-operation between disciplines as different from each other as mathematics, physical education, dance, music and art. It would seem, at first sight, somewhat unlikely that such co-operation should be possible. After all, what has gymnastics to do with mathematics or how are the arts connected with maths?

The movement of the body or parts of the body in space could, upon reflection, at least contribute to that part of mathematics known as geometry. Let us not forget that geometry is the study of the properties of space. How could one better find out properties of space than by moving around in it? And since the only way in which we can move around in space is by using our bodies, we immediately have our first bridge between gymnastics and mathematics. Of course, from time immemorial, fingers have been used for mathematical purposes. In fact, our decimal system of notation is undoubtedly based on the fact that we possess ten fingers. Here is an immediate link between mathematics and the sense of the sense of touch.

Counting is very easily accomplished by stretching out fingers one after the other. In this way, we can count in fives or in tens, and consequently in twenties and so on.

Another obvious connection between mathematics and the body is dance. A dance does not only have spatial properties; it also has a tempo, that is, rhythmical properties. A waltz is a three beat rhythm and so the mathematics surrounding the number three could possibly have some connections with the properties of the waltz.

Different kinds of metre could be associated with different kinds of numerical problems in mathematics. It is also obvious that the choreography of complicated bodily movements formed by a troop of ballet dancers belongs to mathematics as applied to the possibilities of movement that can be employed by the human body or by sets of human bodies working together in co-ordination. Most sports have mathematical properties. Take a tennis court. It is a rectangle divided in certain regular ways, into areas, and the contact between the ball and the ground in different areas determines the score of the player, not to mention contact between the ball and the net or between the ball and the racket. A number of different variations of the game of tennis could be thought out. For example, there is no reason why a tennis court should be rectangular. It could be an equilateral triangle. We shall see later how such variations can be thought out, enjoyed and played.

Then there are very simple childish games such as hopscotch, which have obvious geometrical, as well as numerical, implications. So, upon reflection, it should not really be surprising that a marriage between mathematics and the movement of the body could result in some really interesting and challenging exercises, both from the point of view of flexing the muscles that of mathematical reasoning and reflection.

Our sense of sight allows us to appreciate shape, colour, shading of light and dark and the many ways these aspects of the world interact with each other in the phenomenal world of nature. Such is the stimulus under which we all live, but the artist among us finds ways of digesting these complex inputs. After he has re-formed, re-thought and re-felt them, he puts the results down on canvas or in the shape of a sculpture. Playing with colour and shape, both in a relatively free way and in a more restricted and structured way, could well contribute to an improved understanding of how the world ticks over and what it is made of.

So in this book I shall try to take the reader into some situations in which he will learn some mathematics through moving his body, through touch, through his sense of rhythm, through his appreciation of colour and shape, and finally by showing him how he can personally enjoy the elusive process of abstraction by going through its various stages from the most concrete and simple games to the purest of mathematical abstractions.

1. Dances

Perhaps the most primitive of the senses is the sense of movement. A great deal of the total enjoyment in the world consists of situations in which we move ourselves around from place to place or use our bodies in some way in order to learn and enjoy skills that are possible owing to the way our bodies are built. Dancing is an almost universally enjoyed activity, which can range from the most primitive to the most sophisticated ways of moving about. Now that it is generally agreed that everybody should have the chance of learning all the useful and interesting things that humanity has invented in the past few thousand years, as far as he is able to do so, we should think around for ways in which book-learning, open only to a few, can be replaced by activity-learning, open to all. Since the movement of the body through either dance or other physical exercises is so generally enjoyed, what could be a better introduction to a difficult subject than suitably designed dances which would help to introduce the learner to the subject. Mathematics is generally regarded as very difficult, although it still remains to be seen whether the difficulty does not reside in the way it is dressed up and not in the subject matter itself. So in this volume it is supposed as a prerequisite that most people will enjoy doing mathematical dances, and in the process will learn some considerable amount of mathematics, although such learning could well be regarded as incidental to the enjoyment of the dances and other games suggested.

For the past few years I have been playing around with the possibility of using movement as an essential component of learning mathematics, and as a result quite a few children in the most unlikely places such as Saipan, Kavieng, Goroka, Székesfehérvar, New York and Sherbrooke, are probably at this very moment dancing their way to mathematical competence. Perhaps it is time to stop restricting all this fun to schoolchildren. Mothers, fathers and children could have fun in leisure hours with ideas from books such as this. In what follows I only make suggestions, give the ingredients so to speak, and the reader is then in the position to make up the dances to his own recipe.

The three cornered waltz

Rules referred to dancers

This can be danced by one boy and two girls or one girl and two boys. We shall give instructions for one boy and two girls. So there will be a boy, a first girl and a second girl. Three spaces are chosen on the floor which will be occupied by the three persons. They stand in these places and hold hands, making a circle or, if you like, a triangle. The steps are as follows:

'Right' means go to the space occupied by the person on your right, taking three steps, that is a waltz step.

'Left' means go to the person occupying the space on your left, again doing one waltz step, that is a one-two-three.

The 'boys' twiddle — here the boy and the first girl make an arch and the second girl goes through the arch to occupy the place of the first girl, and the first girl proceeds to occupy the place previously occupied by the second girl.

9

During this manoeuvre, the dancers must not let go of their hands and the boy must twiddle about himself, without letting go of the girls, and finish facing outwards. The whole manoeuvre should be done in two waltz steps, that is, one-two-three, one-two-three, and during this double beat, the two girls will have changed places and will be facing outwards, and, of course, the boy will have stayed in the same place, but will now be facing outwards.

If this step has been correctly carried out, the arms should not be crossed in any kind of knot, but each dancer should be facing outwards instead of inwards. If the boy's twiddle is done well again, the whole procedure is undone, that is, the first girl and the boy make an arch again and the second girl goes through the arch and again the first and the second girls will have changed places and the boy will have twiddled about himself and have finished facing inwards, making a circle or triangle in which all the dancers face towards each other.

In exactly the same way, there can be a first girl's twiddle in which case the first girl twiddles about herself and the second girl and the boy change places, and the second girl's twiddle in which the second girl twiddles about herself and the first girl and the boy change places.

It must be remembered that at no time during the dance must the dancers let go of each other's hands. A twiddle step has the effect of changing the circle from one of facing inwards

Figure 1

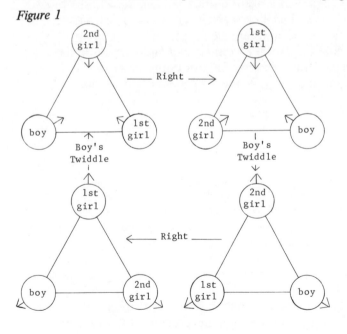

10

into one in which the dancers face outwards, or of changing it from facing outwards into one facing inwards. On the other hand, the left and the right steps will not change the inwards-outwards orientation of the dancers. It will be remembered that if the right move is an anti-clockwise move with the dancers facing inwards, then the right move will become a clockwise move when the dancers face outwards. This is shown on Figure 1. In other words, the moves are not distinguished from one another by being clockwise or anti-clockwise, but by being danced to the right or to the left of the dancers.

With these steps, it will be possible to arrange a number of sequences which will bring the dancers back to their original positions. For example,

right-right-right

obviously will bring them back to their original positions. Equally,

left-left-left

will do so. But, there are others, such as:

any twiddle followed by the same twiddle;

a twiddle, followed by a right, followed by the same twiddle as before, followed by a right.

All the above sequences will bring the dancers back to their original positions. Other sequences are:

boy's twiddle, right, boy's twiddle, right;

boy's twiddle, left, boy's twiddle, left;

first girl's twiddle, right, first girl's twiddle, right.

It is possible to do the left and the right twice followed by the twiddle. For example, one series of steps might be:

11

right, right, first girl's twiddle, right, right, first girl's twiddle.

Another, more interesting possibility, is the following sequence:

boy's twiddle, first girl's twiddle, second girl's twiddle, boy's twiddle, first girl's twiddle, boy's twiddle, first girl's twiddle, second girl's twiddle.

Out of these, certain series of steps could be extracted which can be danced to a three fourths rhythm of any kind.

Rules referred to the dance floor

The rules can also be given in relation to the space which is occupied by the dancers and not to the dancers themselves. It will be noticed that in the instructions given just now, the moves were named after the dancers. The directions in which the steps were to be taken in the left and the right moves depended on which way the dancers were orientated at the time they were to carry out those particular steps.

If we call the positions in which the players have been placed one, two and three, where one, two and three are considered to go around in a clockwise sense, then we may talk about a *one-twiddle* or a *two-twiddle* or a *three-twiddle*. A one-twiddle will mean that whoever is at one is

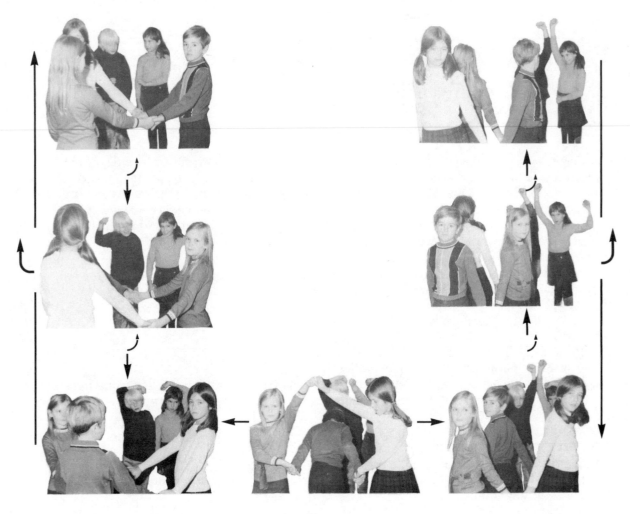

Figure 2

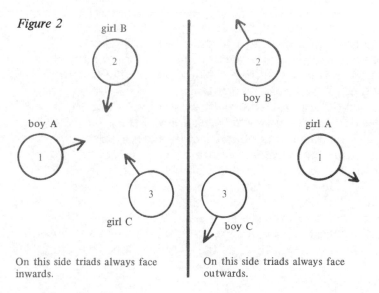

girl B

boy A

girl C

boy B

girl A

boy C

On this side triads always face inwards.

On this side triads always face outwards.

the person who is doing the twiddling and the other two are changing places. Similarly, for the two-twiddle and the three-twiddle. In order to refer the 'rotating' steps to the dance floor, instead of right and left moves, we will speak of clockwise and anti-clockwise moves. In mathematics, this is referred to as using *fixed axes* in space whereas referring to the dancers would be called using axes fixed in the body or *mobile axes*. So, for example, sets of steps taking the dancers back to their original positions could be:

clockwise-clockwise-clockwise instead of left-left-left

and,

anti-clockwise - anti-clockwise - anti-clockwise instead of right-right-right

and so on.

Figure 3

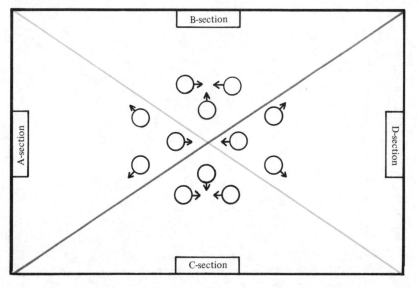

B-section

A-section

D-section

C-section

To make the dance choreographically more interesting, we could dance it with six people. There could be an imaginary line drawn across the floor parallel to which we would draw position three as well as the other position two and the other position three of the other triad of dancers. Positions one, in each case, would be farther away from the line dividing the two triads.

At a certain stage in the choreography the two triads can change over. Now it should be established which persons correspond to each other in the two triads. For example, one triad could be two boys and a girl and the other triad could be two girls and a boy. Each girl or boy in one triad would have a partner of the opposite sex in the other triad. Each person would always have to occupy the position which is the reflection of his partner's position across the imaginary line, that is, if a person is in position one, in one triad, his partner in the other triad must be in position one marked on the other side of the imaginary line. Now, while we are changing over and going across the imaginary line and occupying the opposite triad's place, in each triad the two members of the same sex will have to make an arch and the remaining dancer will have to go through the arch and so the orientation towards the inside will then be exchanged for an orientation towards the outside and an orientation towards the outside will be changed into an orientation towards the inside.

Figure 4

all   the   way   round

This change can usually be accomplished in four waltz steps. If this does not seem to be enough, six or eight steps can be allowed for the change over. The game could be extended to four triads where there are two lines at right angles, let us say the red line and the green line, and on each side of the red line there are two triads and on each side of the green line there are two triads. So, sometimes, the triads exchange with one another across the red line and sometimes they exchange with one another across the green line. Or, they may simply waltz over to the next quarter of the floor in a clockwise sense. Or, they may waltz over to the next quarter in a counter-clockwise sense and so on.

So, quite interesting choreographical effects can be obtained by using one of eight different ways by which one can go from one place to another. These are the following:

Let A and B be on one side of the red line and C and D on the other side so that A is opposite C across the red line and B is opposite D across the red line. Then we have the following possibilities for exchanging the four triads:

pairs of triads exchange across the red line;

pairs of triads exchange across the green line;

A and D change places while B and C change places (this can be accomplished by them dancing half way around to their appropriate corners; this will avoid them colliding with one another.)

A fourth possibility is for them to dance all the way around and regain their previous quarter of the floor;

another possibility is for them to dance a quarter of the way, clockwise;

another, a quarter of the way anti-clockwise;

then, we may have A and D changing places while B and C simply waltz around in their own places;

lastly, we could have B and C changing places while A and D waltz around in their own quarters.

Naturally, there are many other possibilities for changing but there is no need, at this stage, to make the game too complicated. The kinds of exchanges between the triads which we have suggested correspond to the ways in which a square can be moved from position to position while covering the same surface area of the floor. To make sure that no others than the ones that have been described are carried out, a cardboard or a wooden square may be used, the corners of which may be marked A, B, C and D, on both sides of the square, so that there is a corner of the square which is known as the A corner and another corner is known as the B corner and a third one opposite A will be C and then opposite B will be D. The moves which will twiddle or turn the square over into other positions in which it will continue to occupy the same space on the floor, will be seen to produce exactly the exchanges or moves from quarters to other quarters of the triads of dancers which we have described.

The four-cornered dihedral reel

Rules referred to the dancers

This can be danced by four dancers. In effect, the moves have already been described under the heading of *Moving the Triads Around the Dance Floor* as shown diagrammatically in Figure 3, except that there the steps are referred to the floor. Let us say we have a first girl and a second girl and a first boy and a second boy. Suppose that the first girl and the first boy are partners and the second boy and the second girl are partners.

The dancers hold hands and stand in four chosen places, forming approximately the four corners of a square. The moves are done in a four-fourths rhythm, that is, you count one-two

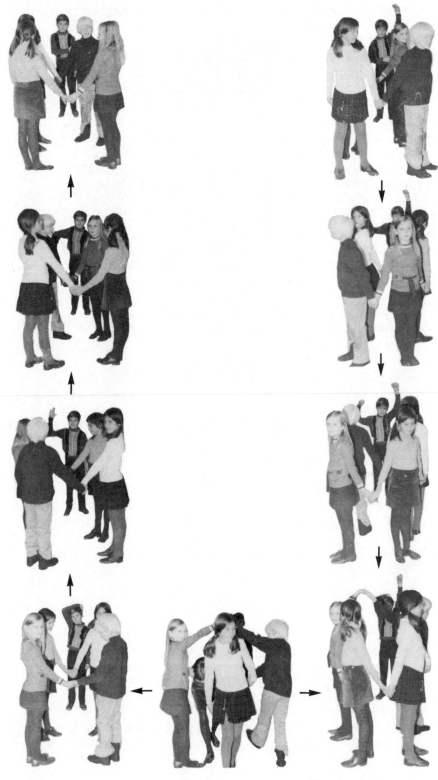

three-four instead of the waltz rhythm which is one-two-three, one-two-three. The dancers do not let go of each others hands during the steps.

In this game also there is a right move and a left move, in which you move to the right to a one-two-three-four rhythm or to the left to a one-two-three-four rhythm, each time reaching the next space.

Next there is the move in which each dancer changes places with his or her partner. This means that the first boy and the first girl change places and the second boy and the second girl change places. Now, this can either happen by the girls making an arch and the boys going through it or by the boys making an arch and the girls going through it. The dancers must not let go of each other's hands. There might at the start be a certain amount of un-twiddling to do in order to untangle the knots into which the arms are likely to get as a result of this step. Again, facing inwards will be replaced by facing outwards and facing outwards by facing inwards.

Next, there are the moves in which ones and twos change places, in which case, again, either the ones make an arch for the twos to go through or the twos make an arch for the ones to go through.

Naturally, it is possible to add two more moves, one in which the dancers dance all the way around and another in which they dance half way around. So, dancing half way around will be equivalent to a left-left or a right-right and the dancing all the way around would be equivalent to a left-left-left-left or else a right-right-right-right. So, it is seen, that these and other sequences of steps will bring dancers back to their original places in the same way as this was the case with the waltz. For example, apart from a left-left-left-left and the obvious right-right-right-right that will take everyone back to his own starting point, we shall also have the following types of sequences:

left, partners change, left, partners change;
right, partners change, right, partners change;
left, one-two change, left, one-two change;
right, one-two change, right one-two change.

It is also possible to take not just a left or a right but a left-left or a right-right-right or a left-left-left and combine them with the cross-over moves to get back to the original starting point.

For example, left-left-left, partners change, left-left-left, partners change, will take everybody back to where they started.

Rules referred to the dance floor

Again, it will be seen that it will be possible to define all these steps in terms of positions on the dance floor instead of in the way they have been defined, namely with reference to the actual people who have been doing the dancing. Instead of saying that the partners change, we could say that the people standing across the red line change, if we draw a red line on the floor. The red line could remain imaginary. Instead of 'move to the right to occupy the space where the nearest person is', you could say, 'move clockwise or move anti-clockwise to the space occupied by the nearest person in that direction'.

So, the whole dance can be explained in terms of steps referred to the dance floor or moves referred to the people doing the dancing as the case may be. In the first case we have a fixed frame of reference; in the second we have a moving frame of reference because we are referring the moves to the dancers themselves, who are, of course, moving, whereas in the first case we would be referring the dance steps to the dance floor, which is not moving.

To complete the dance moves, we would really have to have two more steps in order to imitate what can happen to a square when you pick it up from the floor and put it down again so as to occupy the same space as it did before. We have no move yet for our dancers that corresponds to picking up the square, holding it along a diagonal and twiddling it over the other side. This would mean that the people who corresponded to the corners where we pick the square up would not move; they would stay where they were and the other two across the other diagonal would change over. This is rather difficult to do without letting go of hands so possibly an exception could be made here. This means that one pair of opposites across one diagonal could dance over and change with each other and the ones who do not change could do a pirouette or some such. It is, however, possible to do this change by making an arch, everybody going through the arch and the last person twiddling about himself.

Another way of doing it would be for an arch to be made by the two people who are not going to move and, of the people who have to change places across the other diagonal, one would step over the arch and one would go under it.

In the case of a mobile frame of reference, the diagonal would be fixed by taking two *persons* diagonally opposite who would not move. In the case of a *fixed frame,* we would fix two spaces.

Extensions to more dancers

Variations on both of the last dances can be introduced by having six people instead of three in the circle for the waltz and eight people instead of four in the four-cornered dihedral reel.

In the case of the waltz, instead of one person not moving out of place, we would now have two persons not moving out of place, namely two persons who were opposite one another. That could be a boy and a girl who are supposed to be partners in the dance, but, of course, they are never together because they are always opposite, separated by two other dancers. In this case, we would have to have the sequence boy-girl-boy-girl-boy-girl, making up the circle; each boy would have a girl opposite him and each girl would have a boy opposite her. So, we would have a first couple a second couple and a third couple. The steps could then be called 'first couple cross-over' which means that the first couple stays still and the others have to cross over. In the same way this can be generalized to the foursome dance, making it into an eightsome dance.

Figure 5

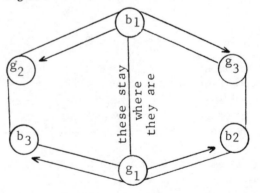

A 'right' would take each boy to the place occupied by the next boy on his right and each girl to the next girl on her right and the same would apply to the left.

Here is a possible series of moves:

Figure 6

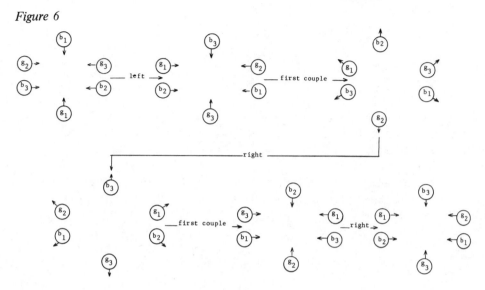

Here is one for the eightsome dihedral:

Figure 7

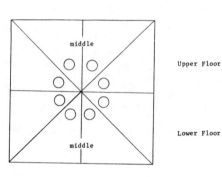

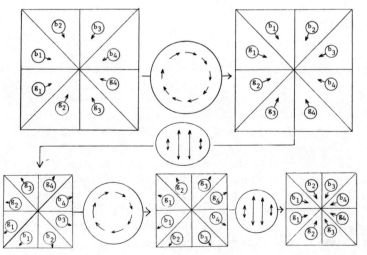

Figure 8

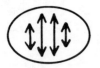

In Fig.8 above, the steps are referred to the dance floor and the step is carried out by either the two upper middle ones making an arch and the lower side ones going through it, followed by the others or by the lower middle ones making an arch and the upper middle ones going through it, followed by the others.

Many other such steps may be thought out. If in a step *all* dancers must cross a certain line, then either couple astride the line perpendicular to the line to be crossed may make the arch for the others to go through (see fig.9).

Figure 9

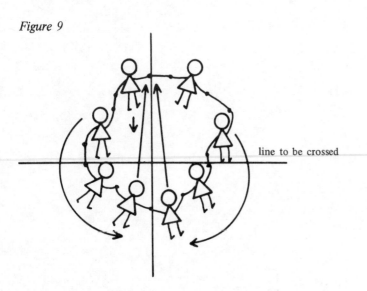

line to be crossed

Above is a sketch of how this can be done.

The reader is assured that the steps can all be carried out without letting go of hands in any of the above cases.

In the case of the six person dance, the steps can be worked out by considering an equilateral triangle in which the boys are the vertices and the girls are at the mid-points of the opposite sides. So, clearly, if one boy is at a vertex and his partner is at the mid-point of the opposite side, then if they do not move, that means that that triangle has to be twiddled about the line joining that vertex to that mid-point and replaced on the floor so as to occupy the same space as before. This means that the two other vertices and the two other mid-points will have to change places with each other in position. The same applies to the square where, instead of having just four dancers identified with the four corners of the square, we can also have the four mid-points of the sides of the square built into the game. Again, it will be easy to discover how we can use the two diagonals and the two joins of the mid-points of opposite sides of the square as twiddling

20

axes and from these we can work out the steps for the eightsome dance reel. These will not be the same steps as those shown on the last set of figures, as if we imagine dances at the corners and at the mid-points of sides of squares, for every 'cross-over' there will always be two dancers that stay put. In the figures mentioned nobody stays put.

It is obvious that these dances can be extended to five, six, seven, eight, nine, ten, any number of people with more and more complicated ways of doing the steps. People will, of course, choose for themselves the kind of dance which suits the degree of complexity of what they want to do. The four-cornered reel can, of course, also be danced in two foursomes or four foursomes or even in three foursomes and various exchanges of foursomes can be added to the pattern.

Figure 10

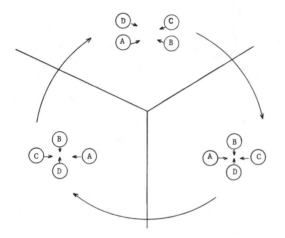

Figure 11

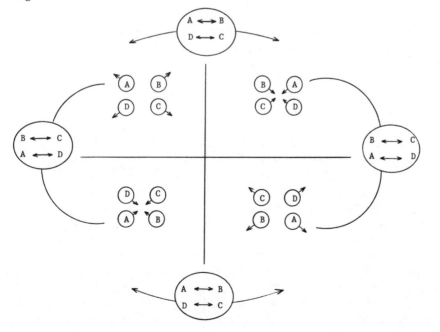

2. Gymnastics with arms and legs

The five-position arm game with outstretched arms

FIRST OF ALL, one has to learn a certain five-cycle. In the O position both arms are down. The position in which the left arm is stretched out horizontally will be called LEFT ONE. The LEFT TWO position will be the one in which the left arm is in the vertical position. The RIGHT ONE position will be the one in which the right arm is stretched out horizontally and the RIGHT TWO position the one in which the right arm is in the vertical position. Now we can make a cycle out of these five different positions in the following order:

both arms down, the O position;
left arm out, LEFT 1 position;
left arm up, LEFT 2 position;
right arm up, RIGHT 2 position;
right arm out, RIGHT 1 position;

after which we return to zero.

Now, the command for going from any one of these positions to the next one *along this cycle,* will be given by the commander when he puts his left arm out in the horizontal position, that is he will show LEFT 1. This means that if you are in the ZERO position you have to move to the LEFT 1, that is you have to move your left arm out horizontally. If your left arm is already horizontal and you received the command LEFT 1, you have to move it into a vertical position. If your arm is already in the vertical position and you receive the command, LEFT 1, you drop this left arm down and put the right arm up in the vertical position. If your right arm is in the vertical position and you receive the LEFT 1 command, you lower it to the horizontal position and from here with the same command, you lower it to the ZERO position.

In other words, LEFT 1, that is the command being issued by jerking the left arm horizontally out, and then dropping it to zero, means that the person obeying must move one space along the cycle just described. Naturally, jerking the right arm out and dropping it is a command to do the cycle in the opposite direction So, for example, if your right arm is vertically up and you receive the command RIGHT 1, that is the commander jerks his right arm out horizontally, then you must drop your right arm from the vertical position and lift the left arm up into the vertical position. This is a move along a cycle in the opposite sense of the first cycle just described.

Naturally the command LEFT 2 will mean that we have to move not to the next but to the one after the next of the positions in the LEFT cycle and RIGHT 2 will mean moving from any position to the next position but one in the right cycle. In this case, one could have four or five people standing and another person standing in front of them but with his back to them. This is so that less confusion should arise about the rights and the lefts as he gives his commands. As the people make mistakes they sit down and the last person to stay in the game wins.

It is possible to make a kind of a screw motion out of this by having several people standing in front of each other in successive positions of the cycle. For example, let the first person in the row of people be in the zero position, the next one in LEFT 1, that is with the left arm stretched out horizontally, the one behind him with the left arm vertical, the one behind him with the right arm vertical, the one behind him with the right arm horizontal and the last one could come down to zero. In this case there are six people in the row but the cycle could naturally continue. Now, in front of the whole row there is the commander who gives the command. Let us say that for quite a considerable length of time he gives the LEFT 1 command. That means everybody has to move one up in the left cycle. This can be done while marching forward. At each step the commander shoots his left arm out and correspondingly, at each step, the people following go from one position to the next. If this is done at a fairly rapid rate, a screw motion effect can be observed when looked at from a distance. Naturally, it is not necessary to do this with the LEFT 1 command being repeated all the time. It can be done with a RIGHT 1 command or with any other. So, for example, one might decide to do ten times LEFT 1 which brings everybody back to their original position (for the second time in succession) and then ten times RIGHT 1 and then, possibly, ten times LEFT 2 and ten times RIGHT 2 and so on.

To complete the commands we can introduce one to be given by zero position. This will be an instruction to do *nothing at all.* In other words, you go on marching without moving your arms into any new positions. To emphasize the zero command, the commander slaps his hands against his thighs on both sides. To emphasize the LEFT 1 command, he dynamically jerks his arm to the left horizontally and drops it to zero. He does likewise with the other commands. So, the command is given by a *dynamic movement* and the positions into which those doing the gymnastics have to change, must follow instantaneously. This can only happen, of course, if the commands are pre-arranged. This is a good opportunity for designing interesting choreographical patterns.

This game can also be done in conjunction with displacements along the floor. Five positions can be marked out and each position can have its associated arm position, that is let us say, at A, B, C, D and E are the positions on the floor marked in the form of five points of a circle. Let us say, at the position A arms have to be down, that is position A means that you have to be in the zero position. In the position B you have to have your left arm horizontal; in C you have to have your left arm vertical; in D you have to have your right arm vertical and in E you have to have your right arm horizontal. So, a movement of the left arm horizontally, that is LEFT 1, as a command, will mean not only a change of the position of the arm from a position to the next one along the left cycle, but also a movement to the appropriate place where this position of the arm is allowed to be shown.

The five-position arm game with arms bent at the elbow

Naturally, it is not necessary to restrict oneself to the positions of the arms given above. More complex positions can also be taken. Two arms may also be used simultaneously instead of just one. Consider the following variation:

the zero position can still be the same as before;
the arm bent at the elbow in front of the body can be LOWER ONE;
the arm bent at the elbow but the part between elbow and shoulder
horizontal and hand downwards can be LOWER TWO.

Then this can be reversed by having hand upwards etc. as seen on the accompanying diagram. These give us the positions UPPER TWO and UPPER ONE.

Figure 12

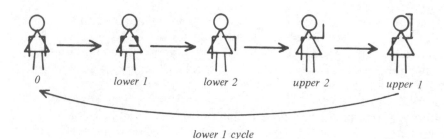

lower 1 cycle

Now, at the beginning, the right arm can be followed by the left arm, that is the right and left arms will always be in the same position. This will always give symmetrical positions with respect to the vertical. To make the game a little more complicated, the left and the right arms could be allowed to move into different positions. Each arm separately would follow the instructions given by the command. The commands would be as follows:

one move in the cycle one way;
two moves in the cycle one way;
one move in the cycle the other way;
two moves in the cycle the other way.

The simultaneous performance of these cycles on the two arms is illustrated again in the following diagrams:

Figure 13

In all these cases *one arm of the commander* was telling *both arms of the gymnast* what to do. Naturally, it could be arranged that the right arm gives the command to the right arm and the left arm to the left arm.

For example:

Figure 15

Gymnast: Commander: Gymnast: Commander: Gymnast: etc.

It has only to be remembered that the LOWER 1 cycle is the following:

Figure 16

Command

The UPPER 1 cycle is the reverse of the above.
The LOWER 2 cycle will be:

Figure 17

Command

The UPPER 2 cycle is the reverse of the above
Naturally, other series of movements would do just as well.

This can also be done by several persons together and some quite interesting tableaux can be generated as shown on the accompanying diagrams:

25

Figure 18

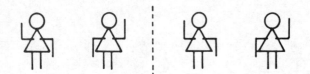

Command:

(meaning one up on either side)

It will be noticed that the symmetry about the middle *has not been spoiled* by the command. However, now let us use an *asymmetrical command* on the last tableau, such as, for example:

Figure 19

(meaning one up on one side and two up on the other)

where we note that the symmetry about the middle is now *spoiled*.

Naturally, it is not necessary to restrict ourselves to cycles of five. Sometimes, it is easier to do a cycle of four or even a cycle of three, as we shall see in some other games.

26

The arm and leg game

'Move the limb shown' game

In this one, we offer the choice of having your right arm in front of you horizontally or your left arm in front of you horizontally or either arm hanging down by the side of your body, as the case may be.

Your right leg could be kicked out horizontally in front of you; your left leg could be kicked out horizontally in front of you. Now, since it is not possible to kick out both the right and the left legs simultaneously in front of you and remain standing, you could sit down to do this exercise first. Thus it is possible to hold right leg, left leg, right arm and left arm in front of you horizontally. It will be seen that each limb has two possible positions:

(i)   in front of you horizontally;
(ii) in the normal relaxed position.

There are 16 different positions in which the body is allowed to be (see Figure 20).

The sixteen positions of the arm and leg game

Figure 20

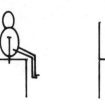  

Figure 21

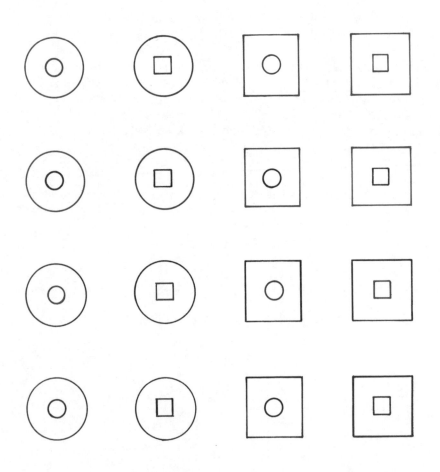

As we move from one position to another above, a change of colour means a change in the position of the leg. A change of shape means a change in the position of the arm. The outside shape shows the right side of the body, the inside shape the left side.

The rules for changing from one position to another are as follows:
The commander or operator will shoot those limbs out which are the ones for the gymnast to move. For example, if the commander shoots out the right arm and the left leg, it means that wherever the gymnast's right arm or left leg happen to be, he has to change them to the other positions in which these limbs are allowed to be. For example, if the *right arm is out* and all the other limbs are down, then a command of **right arm, left leg,** will induce the right arm to go down and the left leg to come out, that is, whatever limbs the commander puts out are the limbs for the gymnast to move.

It is surprising how difficult it is to do this. A certain amount of practice will be necessary before some of the physical exercises which have a geometrical look about them can be done on this basis. Examples are given in the diagrams below:

Figure 22

Start	Command	Finish-Start	Command	Finish

Gymnast	Command	Gymnast	Command	Gymnast

and so on.

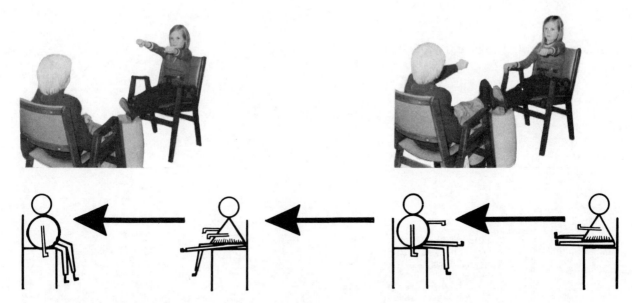

It will be seen that if the same limb is stretched out in the case of the gymnast as well as of the commander, the FINISH will see that limb *down*. If one of them is stretched out and the other not, the FINISH will see that limb *stretched out*. If they are both down, it will be *down* at the FINISH as well. This is one way of remembering quickly how to respond to the commands.

To make the game competitive, if so desired, a group can play together following the same series of commands. As they make mistakes, players fall out, the last winning the game. Or alternatively, each person could take his turn to command, taking, say, a dozen commands each. Then the commander who can induce the players to make the largest number of mistakes wins the game.

Three-cycles

We could introduce three-cycles into the game by changing the coding system for giving the commands. We could give the commander a hat so that when he has a hat on his commands mean one thing and without a hat on they mean another thing. For a start, let us go back to giving the commands with one side of the body only. The commands will be carried out by both sides of the gymnast's body, i.e. by his right arm and leg as well as by his left arm and leg. There are four positions in which one side of the body can be. These are:

Figure 23

zero   arm   leg   armleg

Let us try the following command-code:

Figure 24

Command:

Resulting State of Affairs:
Move to ZERO position, i.e.
both arms down,
both legs down.

Stay as you are.
(This has the same effect as:

Figure 24

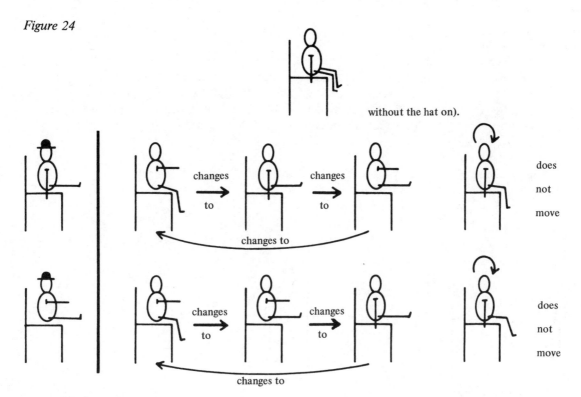

without the hat on).

which means that a
    zero command

brings you back to the zero position from
wherever you happen to be (you go to jail);

    arm command

tells you to stay where you are;

    leg command

tells you to move
from arm position to leg position,
from leg position to armleg position,
from armleg position to arm position;

    armleg command

tells you to move
from arm position to armleg position,
from armleg position to leg position,
from leg position to arm position;

as the diagrams above indicate.

A typical three-cycle generated by, for example, the *leg command* would be the following:

Figure 25

31

If we follow the series in fig. 23 from right to left, we shall see that it is an
armleg command
which is generating the three-cycles.

The hat-commands can be likened to a *multiplication,* where multiplication by zero invariably results in a zero-situation. The arm-command with the hat on corresponds to multiplying by 1. The leg command may be likened to some other non-trivial multiplication where the armleg command could therefore be likened to the corresponding *division.*

The non-hat commands can be conceived to be *additions,* in which
like limb-positions cancel out
instead of 'opposites cancelling out' as they do in conventional algebra
We have:

Figure 26

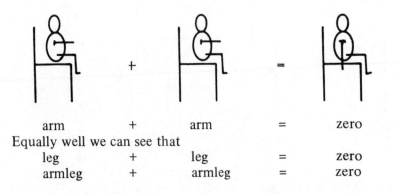

arm	+	arm	=	zero

Equally well we can see that

leg	+	leg	=	zero
armleg	+	armleg	=	zero

It is also easy to see that if we 'add' any two of the following:
arm, leg, armleg,
we obtain the remaining one. Finally, 'adding zero' has no effect.
For example:

Figure 27

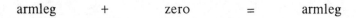

armleg	+	zero	=	armleg

In this way both the 'addition gymnastics' and the 'multiplication gymnastics' are quite easy to learn.

The arm and leg game could also be played on a four by four grid as shown in Figure 18, or, of course, the arrangement of the positions could be quite different, for example:

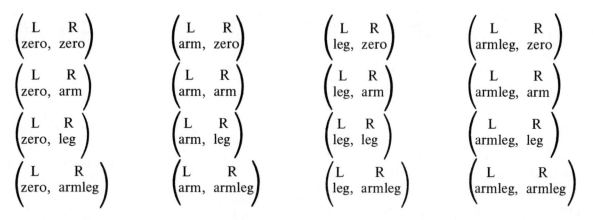

$$\begin{pmatrix} \text{L} \quad \text{R} \\ \text{zero, zero} \end{pmatrix} \quad \begin{pmatrix} \text{L} \quad \text{R} \\ \text{arm, zero} \end{pmatrix} \quad \begin{pmatrix} \text{L} \quad \text{R} \\ \text{leg, zero} \end{pmatrix} \quad \begin{pmatrix} \text{L} \quad \text{R} \\ \text{armleg, zero} \end{pmatrix}$$

$$\begin{pmatrix} \text{L} \quad \text{R} \\ \text{zero, arm} \end{pmatrix} \quad \begin{pmatrix} \text{L} \quad \text{R} \\ \text{arm, arm} \end{pmatrix} \quad \begin{pmatrix} \text{L} \quad \text{R} \\ \text{leg, arm} \end{pmatrix} \quad \begin{pmatrix} \text{L} \quad \text{R} \\ \text{armleg, arm} \end{pmatrix}$$

$$\begin{pmatrix} \text{L} \quad \text{R} \\ \text{zero, leg} \end{pmatrix} \quad \begin{pmatrix} \text{L} \quad \text{R} \\ \text{arm, leg} \end{pmatrix} \quad \begin{pmatrix} \text{L} \quad \text{R} \\ \text{leg, leg} \end{pmatrix} \quad \begin{pmatrix} \text{L} \quad \text{R} \\ \text{armleg, leg} \end{pmatrix}$$

$$\begin{pmatrix} \text{L} \quad \text{R} \\ \text{zero, armleg} \end{pmatrix} \quad \begin{pmatrix} \text{L} \quad \text{R} \\ \text{arm, armleg} \end{pmatrix} \quad \begin{pmatrix} \text{L} \quad \text{R} \\ \text{leg, armleg} \end{pmatrix} \quad \begin{pmatrix} \text{L} \quad \text{R} \\ \text{armleg, armleg} \end{pmatrix}$$

It will be seen that to perform a three-cycle either we have to do so entirely in the first column or entirely in the first row, or else if we once begin elsewhere, the three members of the three-cycles will all come from different rows *and* columns. If we denote arm by 1, leg by 2 and armleg by 3, the remaining nine positions, which are not either in the first row or in the first column, are as follows:

$$(1,1) \qquad\qquad (2,1) \qquad\qquad (3,1)$$

$$(1,2) \qquad\qquad (2,2) \qquad\qquad (3,2)$$

$$(1,3) \qquad\qquad (2,3) \qquad\qquad (3,3)$$

Three cycles would be the following:

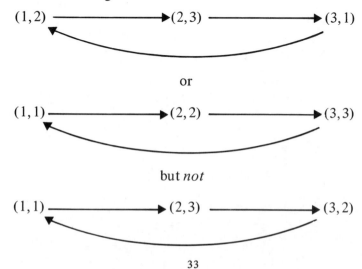

$$(1,2) \longrightarrow (2,3) \longrightarrow (3,1)$$

or

$$(1,1) \longrightarrow (2,2) \longrightarrow (3,3)$$

but *not*

$$(1,1) \longrightarrow (2,3) \longrightarrow (3,2)$$

because in the latter cycle the left side of the body does the cycle:

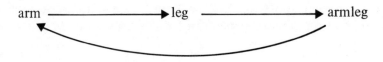

while at the same time the right side of the body does the cycle:

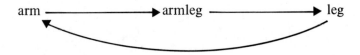

The nine-position arm game

Consider the following positions:

Figure 28

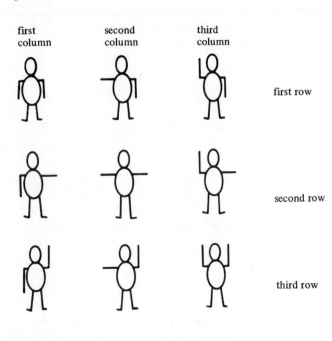

which could be denoted by the symbols:

(down, down), (middle, down), (up, down)

(down, middle), (middle, middle), (up, middle)

(down, up,), (middle, up,), (up, up,)

We can immediately see that there are the following cycles:

Figure 29

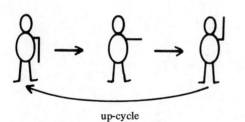
up-cycle

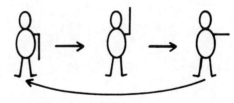
down-cycle

these being the opposites of each other,

and

Figure 30

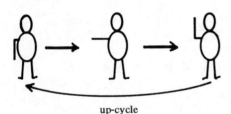
up-cycle

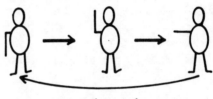
down-cycle

Each of these involves the movement of one side of the body only and can be seen to correspond to movements along the rows or along the columns of the nine positions. Naturally, the cycles can be mixed with each other, so that we move the left arm as well as the right arm. So, the rules giving the cycles would be:

> left arm does not move, right arm does up-cycle;
>
> left arm does not move, right arm does down-cycle;
>
> left arm does up-cycle, right arm does not move;
>
> left arm does down-cycle, right arm does not move;
>
> left arm does up-cycle, right arm does up-cycle;
>
> left arm does up-cycle, right arm does down-cycle;
>
> left arm does down-cycle, right arm does up-cycle;
>
> left arm does down-cycle, right arm does down-cycle;

We can establish a way of coding the commands as follows:

Figure 31

do nothing;

left nothing, right down;

left down, right up;

left up, right nothing;

left nothing, right up;

left down, right down;

left down, right nothing;

left up, right down;

left up, right up;

Some cycles, generated by repeating the same command a number of times, would be, for example:

Figure 32, 33

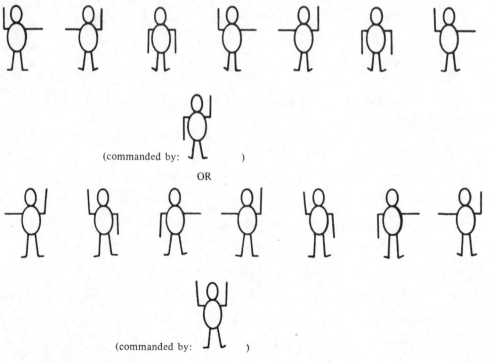

(commanded by:)

OR

(commanded by:)

A row of gymnasts could stand side by side or behind one another, possibly all at different positions and the series of commands would result in interesting rotatory motions. In fact, the commands could be issued to each of nine different gymnasts simultaneously, arranged in the three by three array of page 39. We could also introduce the hat-variant of the commands. The operations so far could be considered the 'additions' and the 'hat-commands' will again be treated as 'multipliers'.

Figure 34

gymnast assumes   position

gymnast does not change position

gymnast changes arm positions from *up* to *down,* or from *down* to *up,* but leaves an outstretched arm where it is

For example, take the following 'multiplications':

Figure 35

It goes without saying that any other three arm-positions would have done just as well for the above exercises. For example:

Figure 36

or even the right and the left could be different from each other and so we would obtain possibilities such as:

Figure 37

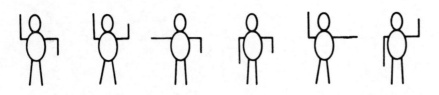

and so on.

Logical considerations

The learning of logic is becoming very much the vogue these days. Even in some elementary school programmes it is beginning to be suggested that logic should be learnt. Whether this is good or bad, of course, very much depends on how it is done.

Naturally, the kind of abstract logic that is learnt at universities is only digestable by the select few, but the kind of logic we use every day is, in fact, digested by most of us if we succeed in life. In a way, this is why we succeed because we are able to, possibly sometimes unconsciously, analyse situations in life, see the logic in them and act appropriately.

So possibly, it might be an idea to look and see what the components are of such logical thinking. If logic is learnt in a fun way by children, it is both useful and pleasurable. A child never asks, as a matter of fact, what a thing is used for as long as he enjoys it. In the programmes where logic is treated as a fun game, children do, in fact, learn it, and they do not ask why.

Here is one possible game. We need eight or nine persons to play in this game. Let us say there is father and mother, uncle and aunt, and four children. Let us call the children Anne, Betty, Charles and Eric. We can take three pieces of rope and put them out in the form of the Ballantine sign found on beer bottles. This is better known in mathematics as a Venn diagram but we can call it a Ballantine diagram if we wish. This consists of two circles interlaced by a third circle underneath or above, depending which way we are looking at the bottle. Let us say that the adults, that is father, mother, uncle and aunt are going to wear hats, just to be able to distinguish them from the children. If there are eight children playing the game, of course, four of them can be wearing hats so as to distinguish them from the children not wearing them. Now let us say, that some children are going to put their right arms up, others are going to put their left arms up, others again are going to have them both up, and others are going to have them both down. This will be the case for those wearing hats as well as for those not wearing hats. We need eight people at least, and the ninth person to lead the game. Let us say that Anne has her right arm up, and her left arm down.

Figure 38

Anne

Uncle

Betty

Aunt

Charles

Father

Eric

Mother

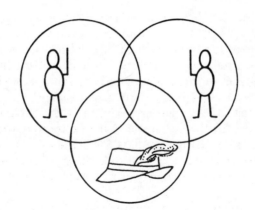

Betty has her left arm up, and her right arm down. Charles has both arms up, and Eric has both arms down. Then, let us think about father, mother, uncle and aunt. Father has both arms up. Mother has both arms down. Uncle has the right arm up, and the left arm down; and aunt has the left arm up, and the right arm down. How, can we give the circles, in the Ballantine diagram, names? The left circle could be for those people who have their right arm up, the right circle could be for those who have their left arm up, or the other way around if we wish. The lower or upper circle could be for those with hats on, or for those without hats on, as we may choose; but let us have them in the lower circle with hats on. In that case, we might have the following situation in the diagram.

Figure 39

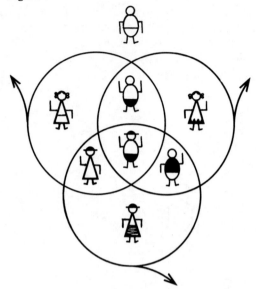

It will be seen that one person, namely Eric, will be out of the circles altogether, because he does not have a hat on, he does not have his right arm up, and he does not have his left arm up either. All the other people will be in at least one circle. There will be one person, namely father, who will be in the three circles right in the middle of the Ballantine picture. Now, it will be quite fun just to find your places in the diagram, and then of course, it will be interesting to recast the names for the circles and finding your new places.

For example, instead of the left circle being for the right arm, and the right circle for the left arm, we could now have the left circle for the left arm and the right circle for the right arm; leaving the hats as they are. Or we may change the hats for the non-hats, and so on. The last person to find his or her correct place could be said to loose a point. The person who has lost the least number of points, after let us say five 'goes' of the game, wins the game.

Another way of playing the game is for a ninth person to come in, observe exactly how the people are situated within the diagram, after which he would turn away. While he is not looking, one of the people would change his position or would give the hat to somebody else, who was not supposed to have it. Then the person would look on again, and would have to correct the mistake. In other words, he would pass the hat to where it belongs, or change the position of the arms if they were wrong, or tentatively change the position of the person if he is wrong, and so on.

If we have not enough space for this kind of game, we do not have to play it with people, we can play it with things. For example, we could take a piece of cardboard and draw the diagrams on it. Then take some objects, such as pencils or pens. Some of the pencils could be long, others short and some of the pens long and others short. We can also have red pencils, and green pencils, and red pens, and green pens. There will again be eight kinds of objects, four kinds of pencils, long red, short red, long green, short green and the same kinds of pens as well. We can decide that one circle is for the red ones, another circle is for the long ones, and another circle is for the pencils.

The game can be played as before or better still, the two games can be played together so that, for instance, father, mother, uncle and aunt take the pens and the children take the pencils. The ones with the right arm up take the long things and the ones with the left arm up take the red things. Each person then has one and only one object, according to this correspondence.

There is no need to play the game with a Ballantine diagram. It is possible to play it with a 'tree'. Let us take eight chairs and put them in a row. We mark a spot in front of the first and the second chair, in front of the third and fourth, in front of the fifth and sixth, and in front of the seventh and the eighth; but not too near the chairs. If we have a piece of masking tape, or rope, or anything else that we might use, for putting temporarily on the floor, we could make a 'branch' or a 'road', from the spots just marked to the corresponding chairs; from the first spot marked we would stick masking tape on the floor to the first chair as well as to the second chair. From the second spot marked, we shall have a road going to the third chair as well as to the fourth chair, and so on. This means that each of the four points marked on the floor will be the point of a 'fork' where a decision has to be made whether we take a right-hand road or a left-hand road.

Now, let us move back away a bit, further away again from the chairs and mark another position between the first and second point and yet another one between the third and the fourth point. We might call these A and B, respectively, just to have a name for them. Let us put some masking tape down from A to the first point, as well as from A to the second point. Then from B to the third point, as well as from B to the fourth point. We should now have made the following construction:

Figure 40

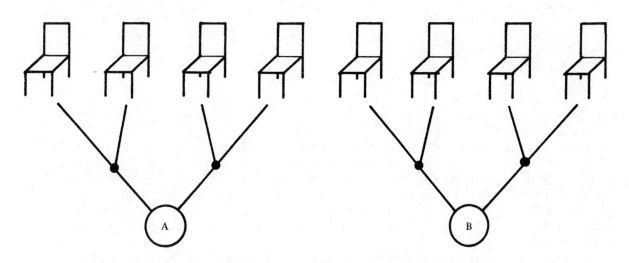

We have two trees, one starting from A, one starting from B. Each tree starts with two branches. At the next branching point again each branch branches off into two more branches. To complete the tree we need to come a little further back between A and B, still further away from the chairs. We mark one more point at the very base of the tree and mark the road from here to A as well as from here to B.

41

Figure 41

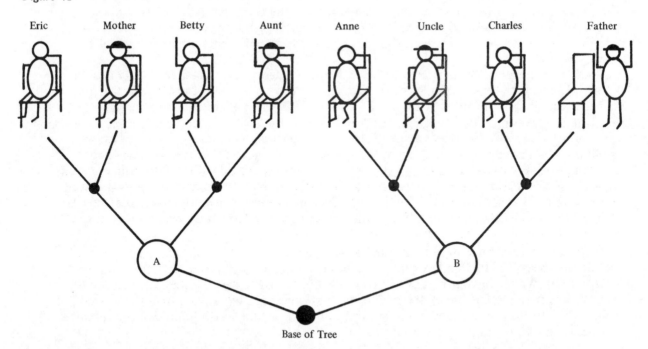

In order to get to any particular chair, along this system of roads, we need *three successive decisions*. Before we start, we have to decide whether we have to go right or left. When we get to the next fork, we again have to decide whether to go right or left. These three decisions could be made to correspond to the three properties we have used, such as right arm up, left arm up, and hats. The first decision could be that your right arm is up. Then you go towards the left if it is not. As the second decision, we could take the left arm, that is if your left arm is up then you go towards the right, and if your left arm is not up then you go towards the left. Finally, at the third decision, we might say that if anyone has a hat on, he goes towards the right, and if not, he goes towards the left.

Counting from right to left, we have father, Charles, uncle, Anne, aunt, Betty, mother and Eric. Again poor Eric comes off worst if the right hand side of the tree is supposed to be the best part, which it would be since it is being led by father; he being head of the family. Again the same exchanging games can be played. Somebody puts the hat somewhere else, or somebody messes up the arms, after which a person has to look and see what the mistake is. The person who makes the least number of mistakes wins the game ...

Naturally, it is not necessary to keep the order of the decisions the same. Instead of the right arm up for the first decision, we could have hat or no hat. Then we would have all the adults on the right-hand side of the tree and all the children on the left, because the adults all have hats on.

How the arms are arranged would depend on whether we take the right-hand arm as the second decision and the left-hand arm as the third, or the left-hand arm as the second decision and the right-hand arm as the third. In the first case we would have people next to each other with the right-hand arm up and the right-hand arm down. In the second case it would be the left-hand arm people that would be neighbours on the pairs of chairs which are at the top of the tree.

If we wish to go into any more logic of an explicit nature, we can begin to take people off the tree, or out of the Ballantine diagram. Let us say that it is time to get some coffee and cookies. Auntie asks Betty to come to the kitchen with her while the rest of them are straining their logical muscles to learn some more.

We have now created what is known in logic or language study as a *conditional situation.* It will be seen that anybody who has not his right arm up, does not have his left arm up either. So the condition is:

If not right arm up then not left arm up.

But it is interesting to see equally well that among the people left playing the game:
if a left arm is up, then the right arm is also up.

If left then right is a true property of the set of people left behind, but also, *if not right then not left* is such a true property. It is clearly not true that anybody that has his right arm up also has his left arm up, because among the right arm up people there are some left arm up and there are some left arm down people. So *everything* is not true. This is what makes logices interesting. You cannot conclude everything. In a conditional situation you can, however, conclude *something.* The trick is to find out what kinds of things you can conclude out of the evidence before you. This is what we all have to learn if we wish to draw correct conclusions out of the evidence that is presented to us in any given instruction.

Now let us say that Auntie and Betty have come back. In the meantime there has been a snowstorm and father has to go outside to dig the snow to get his car out. So father and son, say Charles, have to go out and dig the snow together so that father does not get a heart attack. We have now made a different *conditional situation.* What are the conditions now? Clearly:

if you have your right arm up, then you do not have your left arm up, because the only ones allowed to have both up have just gone out to dig the snow.

Is there another condition which is again satisfied by the remaining people now in the room, including Auntie and Betty? Clearly:

if you have your left arm up, then you do not have your right arm up.

The two conditions that are true now are:
if right then non-left,
and
if left then non-right.

Some of you may already be wondering whether there is not some kind of rule knocking around here of a *logical character.* The mathematical reader will recognize what is known as the contrapositive. It is a kind of inversion of a situation but not quite! This is where an awful lot of people confuse the *contrapositive* with what is known as a *converse.* For example, somebody might be arguing that all politicians are rogues and so somebody might reply 'Yah, you are a rogue, so you must be a politician'. Now, of course, there is something wrong with this argument as some of you may already feel. What is wrong with the argument? The argument says that some

if you are a politician then you are a rogue,
not
if you are a rogue then you are a politician.

If politicians are all rogues, it does not mean that all rogues are politicians. Therefore from the information that somebody is a rogue it certainly does not follow that he is a politician even if we assume that all politicians are rogues. But if we do assume the universal true statement that all politicians are rogues

if somebody turns out to be a politician then we can conclude correctly that he is a rogue.

It is not that he is a rogue which is correct; it is the *conclusion* which is correct. We are able to reason correctly from the assumption that all politicians are rogues, and from the fact that he is a politician, that he is a rogue. But we cannot correctly reason from 'all politicians are rogues' and from the fact that 'he is a rogue', that 'he is a politician', although he may well be a politician, but it will not *follow* from what we have been given. In other words, although something may be *true,* it may not *follow* from what we are given to assume.

This kind of thing is very important in the practice of law. You may be guilty, but if the court is not able to prove it, you are let off. What does follow of course is that if all politicians are rogues then all non-rogues are non-politicians! This is the kind of thing we have been looking at in the present situation with the eight chairs and the eight people. We found that while Auntie and Betty were making the coffee, before father and Charles went out to dig the snow that if your right arm was up then your left arm was up and if your left arm was not up, then your right arm was not up either. Substitute for *'right arm is up', 'to be a politician'* and a substitute for *'Left arm is up' 'to be a rogue'* and you have the same argument as we had about the politician.

The game can be played in less structured ways as well. We could have more than eight people and there would be two sides picked. Let us say we have side A and side B playing against each other, playing the right arm up, left arm up game. Then side A would decide quietly without telling anybody in Side B that anybody with a hat on must never put his left arm up, otherwise they can be in any position whatsoever. Then it is up to side B to guess the conditions that have been imposed. They would have to be able to state that if you have a hat on, then you do not have your left arm up, or alternatively, that if you do have your left arm up then you do not have a hat on. If you want to make the game stricter, then knowing *both the above conditions* may be required before the other side wins the point; or may be if they get one of the conditions they win one point, if they get both the conditions they win two points. Next, it is up to the side B to arrange themselves into a situation in which there is a condition to be satisfied and side A have to guess what that is and so on ... The side that wins the most points wins the game. Naturally, there is no need to restrict ourselves to arms up, arms down, hat on, and hat off, many different bodily positions can be used; for instance sitting down, standing up, leaning down, lying down, pulling a face, holding your ear; all sorts of different gestures and positions can be brought in to make the game funnier.

If we wish to make the game even more complicated from the point of view of logic, then instead of sending two people out, from the same pair of chairs, we just send one person out; now what are the two conditions that we have imposed on the situation? The first one is much easier to see than the second. Let us say that the person with the hat on and both the arms down goes out. It is obvious, in this case, that if you have both the arms down, then you do not have a hat on in other words you are a child. 'Both' of course is short for 'left and right' that is logically speaking, we would have to say: if you are looking for a person who at the same time has *left arm not up and right arm not up, then* he will have *no hat* because there are only two people with both arms not up and the one with the hat on has gone to the kitchen, or to see the baby.

The other condition is, that if you do not have a hat on, then either one or the other of your arms must be up. So the situation is somewhat more interesting, even though more complicated. Let us recap:

The first condition now is if both arms down, then no hat; the second condition if hat, then either one or the other arm must be up.

We note that in logic *either one or the other* includes the possibility of *both* being up.

Relationships between 'both' 'either or' and 'and' are at the basis of some very important logical facts. The mathematical reader will recognize them as the germs of what he has learned as the De Morgan rules in his logic course at the University.

Let us play another game to make these rules a lot clearer. Try to construct the following two roads systems on the floor. On the first one, the left-hand road is for those with the left arm up, and the right-hand road is obviously for those with the left arm not up. The right-hand road comes to another fork in which the left-hand fork will be for the right arm up, and for the right-hand fork for the right arm not up. These are the ones that arrive at the final tree, where those that do arrive find their own places on the tree. On the actual tree the first decision is between the left arm being up or down, and the second decision is between the right arm being up or down.

Now let us look at the second diagram. Here, the right-hand fork is taken by the left arm up, and, of course the left-hand fork by the left arm down. The left-hand road meets another fork in which the right-hand road is taken by the right arm up, and the left-hand road by the right arm down. This road joins the previous right-hand road and both these arrive at the final tree where again the decision is made in the following order:

first decision left arm up, or down;

second decision right arm up, or down.

Figure 42

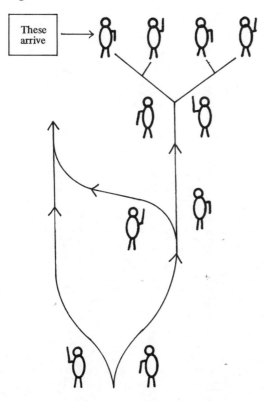

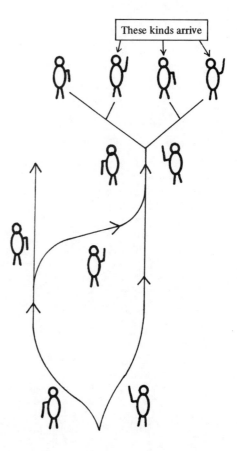

45

It will be seen that on the first tree only one kind of person arrives, namely the kind that has both arms down.

In the second diagram, three types of person arrive. Here you can arrive as long as you have at least one of your arms up. The first diagram is an embodiment of *both arms down,* the 'both' idea being realized. On the right-hand diagram we have either one or the other arm or both up. We make a convention in logic that when we say *either or,* we include the *both.* This makes logic much simpler. So for the right-hand tree, we can say that we will reach the right-hand tree through this network of roads, if we have either one or the other of our arms up. We will reach the left-hand road, if we have both our arms down.

There is no space in this chapter to develop further the logical relation underlying these games. The reader is referred to the book list at the end of the book.

We have presented some *structured games* for learning logical concepts. These games can be played with different materials and the comparisons made, and this way the common essence or *abstraction* hiding behind the activities can be teased out. The 'road-works' and 'trees' introduce the type of more abstract representation which we can then study in its own right to develop the *language of logic.* Thus the road to the learning of logic will be seen to be very similar to the road to the learning of other parts of mathematics, as we hope to show in the later chapters.

3. Rhythmical games

The universality of rhythm

SO FAR, we have been considering bodily activities which make use of the ability of the human person to explore the space around him. In the case of dances, this was done by certain types of displacements, that is, certain types of dance steps that would take you from certain configurations to other configurations. The way we tried to make it fun was by imposing certain restrictions such as not letting go of hands, or doing certain kinds of steps in certain areas of the floor, facing inwards or facing outwards in certain parts of the floor only, and so on. All these were largely dependent on the ability of the person to orientate himself in space. Of course, in the dance we introduced a certain amount of rhythm as well, which brought in time, but this was only by the way. We suggested a waltz rhythm for the games which involved three-cycles and a four fourths rhythm for the games that involved four-cycles. This, of course, is by no means necessary and any other kinds of fancy steps or rhythms could be used in conjunction with these dances.

In the second chapter, we dealt with the exploration of space with arms and legs. There are a number of different positions in which arms and legs can be placed and if these are suitably restricted and certain rules followed, it makes for lively thinking as well as for lively gymnastics.

We tried to combine the exploration of space with a certain amount of reflection on the part of the brain in working out how the rules imposed necessitated certain particular sequences or types of sequences.

In this chapter, we would like to concentrate on the use of rhythms. Now, nature really does abound in rhythm. If there are not many tunes or many spatial regularities in nature, there certainly are many regular rhythms. The whole of nature pulsates with recurring themes: the day and the night, the seasons, the mating cycles of the animal and vegetable kingdoms, even the cycles of the sun spots. There are other cycles on a grander scale such as glaciation and warming up periods in the earth's history, the rotation of the galaxies themselves, and possibly even the pulsation of the entire universe from an original fireball to its most expanded form and its retraction to some future fireball. We may imagine the entire life span of the universe as one beat of expansion and retraction.

On a smaller scale, we have breathing, heart-beating. When we walk we swing our arms and put our legs in front of one another as we move from place to place. Practically everything that we look at in nature has something of the recurring cycles in it and the content of any chain of events which is repeated, is the rhythm. The fact that it is repeated makes it seem rhythmical but the actual rhythm itself, which distinguishes one rhythm from another rhythm, is present in the actual structure of the events themselves.

For example, malaria parasites have sometimes a 24-hour cycle, sometimes a 48-hour cycle and sometimes a 72-hour cycle. Some parasites go through different types of activities even during these cycles of different lengths. Such natural cycles occur in abundance all over nature. The innate longing and love of rhythm in man, presumably, is an attempt to get in touch with the underlying pulse of the structure of events. Whether this is in fact so, or merely a mystical longing, is beside the point. What we do know for a fact is that from the most primitive tribes to the most sophisticated societies, rhythmical movement in the form of dance of all kinds, rhythmical speech in the form of songs and poetry of all kinds, have, from time immemorial, been considered as a most important activity in which human beings can engage and many of the arts are probably some form or another of the application of rhythm. Even the plastic arts do not escape from the necessity to include rhythm; in other words, balance, contrast, proportion, which are all the ingredients of particular rhythms, are found in nature, whence the artist receives his inspiration.

Five-element games

We can beat rhythms out with our fingers or we can step them out with our feet or we can sing them or we can do all of these things.

Let us take our fingers first. We have five fingers and we could associate each finger with one of the notes, do-re-mi-fa-sol. Do would be the thumb, re would be the index finger, mi the middle finger, fa the ring finger and sol the little finger.

Now, let us say that in the first type of rhythmical exercise, we simply go up and down this little five-point scale, that is we go:

```
        sol               sol

    fa      fa         fa      fa

  mi      mi         mi      mi

re          re     re          re

do          do              and so on.
```

We may sing this in certain particular rhythms. For example, we might impose a four-fourths rhythm on this sequence of notes, meaning that a bar would consist of four of these beats, each beat having, for the time being, equal value. So, we could tap the following simple rhythm with our fingers:

do-re-mi-fa / sol-fa-mi-re / do-re-mi-fa / sol-fa-mi-re

and so on. We see that using five fingers, after two bars, we come back to the beginning.

Well, this is not very interesting, so let us try and see what happens when we take six notes in a bar, which could be a six-eighths rhythm. We take for each of the notes the value of *one eighth* and we take six of them. How will our bars follow one another? We will notice that there will be four successive bars of six eighths. These will be the following:

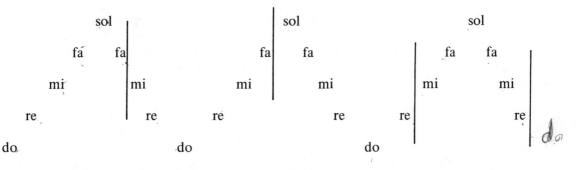

and that would bring us back to do.

Now, naturally, if instead of taking a six eighths rhythm we take three-fourths rhythm, we will have eight bars before coming back to the beginning. Each note will now be considered as a fourth, so we will have:

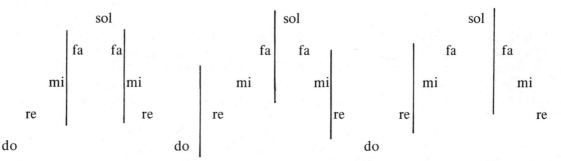

and then we come back to *do-re-mi* at the ninth bar.

In this way, we find an eight-cycle, that is we need eight bars before we come back to the beginning of the cycle. So, depending on the length of the bar, we will get different numbers of bars before the cycle begins to repeat itself.

In order to realize these rhythms, we can beat drums or we can play on the piano or on the guitar, or we can run up and down. In each case we will need five spaces or five notes or five different kinds of drum beat to work on. If we are beating drums, we will need five different kinds of drums or certainly five different kinds of beats on a drum, taking the same length of time. For example:

Figure 43

The only thing that is required is that the same note should be represented by the same rhythm every time it occurs in the cycle. Then, the rhythm or the chain of bars that is obtained in this way, will become noticeable.

Some people might like to do this on drums or with music. Others might like to skip it out. It is also possible, and sometimes enjoyable, to accompany it by arm movements. For example, doh could be the arm crossed over the stomach, ray could be up to the elbow horizontal and elbow to hand vertically down, mi could be the whole arm horizontally, fah could be up to the elbow horizontal and elbow to hand vertically upwards, and soh could be the hand placed on the head making again a right angle at the elbow. The rhythm could, in fact, be reproduced simply by a movement of the arm or arms up and down, through the 'scale':

Figure 44

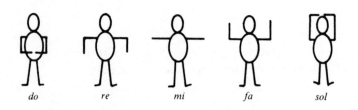

do   re   mi   fa   sol

However, it is more fun to accompany the arm-movement by bodily displacement. We can decide that each of the five spaces occupied would need to have a certain arm position to go with it. We could take the afore-mentioned row of positions which could be called do-re-mi-fa and sol or any other names we like. The names of the children in a family or the names of the dogs and the cats or any other names could also be used to identify the spaces and arm positions.

In this way the rhythms can be walked out or run out back and forth. It must be remembered that do and sol are only stepped on once, that is we do not say:

do-re-mi-fa-sol-sol-fa-mi-re-do-do-re-mi-fa-sol,

but we say:

do-re-mi-fa-sol-fa-mi-re   do-re-mi-fa-sol-fa-mi-re

and so on. That means that as we step on the last position in the row, we take a sudden turn and take our next step onto the position next to the last. We then turn to fa if we have turned around sol and to re if we have turned around at do.

It is also fun to sing the notes. If the rhythm is found to be boring, just taking one-two-three, one-two-three-four or one-two-three-four, one-two-three-four, we could stop on one of the notes and make it even longer or perhaps even twice as long or use it twice. For instance, we could say:

do-re-mi-i ... fa-sol-fa-a ... mi-re-do-o ...

or we could say:

do-re-mi-mi   fa-sol-fa-fa, to the rhythm:

Figure 45

This would create the same cyclic series of events as a waltz rhythm creates, when it is imposed on the five-point scale. However, we have used a different rhythm, in this case an anapest rhythm, an ancient Greek metre. The whole eight-cycle would go like this:

Figure 46

| do-re-*mi*-mi | / | fa-sol-*fa*-fa | / | mi-re-*do*-do | / | re-mi-*fa*-fa |
| sol-fa-*mi*-mi | / | re-do-*re*-re | / | mi-fa-*sol*-sol | / | fa-mi-*re*-re |

and then we come back to the do.

Here are some possible and interesting rhythm combinations that can be done with five notes:

Figure 47

This uses runs of five different notes on a pentatonic scale, the last one repeated to make a more interesting rhythm, and we can see that we obtain a cycle of eight different bars before we get back to the beginning of the cycle.

51

Figure 48

This uses runs of six notes, all of equal value. We arrive back at the 'start' after four different bars.

Let us sum up. If we take five 'elements' and so form an eight cycle such as do-re-mi-fa-sol-fa-mi-re, we come straight back to the original do in just one bar. This is, of course, the least interesting. If we take four elements per bar, then naturally we have:

do-re-mi-fa / sol-fa-mi-re

and we come back to do-re-mi-fa after the second bar.

With six elements we need four bars before we get back to the beginning. We can verify that the same happens with two elements per bar. We have:

do-re / mi-fa / sol-fa / mi-re

and then we are back at the beginning. With odd numbers, that is with one, three, five and seven, it seems to take eight bars to get back to the beginning.

For example, with one per bar we have:

do-re-mi-fa-sol-fa-mi-re:

with three per bar, we have:

do-re-mi / fa-sol-fa / mi-re-do / re-mi-fa / sol-fa-mi / re-do-re / mi-fa-sol / fa-mi-re;

with five per bar, we have:

do-re-mi-fa-sol / fa-mi-re-do-re / mi-fa-sol-fa-mi / re-do-re-mi-fa / sol-fa-mi-re-do / re-mi-fa-sol-fa / mi-re-do-re-mi / fa-sol-fa-mi-re;

and with seven per bar, we have:

do-re-mi-fa-sol-fa-mi / re-do-re-mi-fa-sol-fa / mi-re-do-re-mi-fa-sol / fa-mi-re-do-re-mi-fa / sol-fa-mi-re-do-re-mi / fa-sol-fa-mi-re-do re / mi-fa-sol-fa-mi-re-do / re-mi-fa-sol-fa-mi-re;

Naturally, with nine per bar, we would be back to the same situation as with one and so the cycle repeats itself. We see that interesting regularities can be discovered about the superposition of rhythms on other rhythms. We have been super-imposing different rhythms upon an eight beat rhythm given by our five elements and getting corresponding cycles of bars.

We can see that if there are no common factors different from one, we get the full cycle. We see this when we pit eight against three, eight against five and eight against seven. On the other hand, if there are common factors between the two superimposed cycles, such as between eight and two, eight and six, and eight and four, **we do not get the full cycle.** When we pit eight against two or eight against six, in each case there is a common factor of *two* and so we have a cycle of *four*. When we pit eight against four, there are two common factors, namely two and two and so we get the cycle of *two*.

The reader might start making an intelligent guess about what kind of mathematics is being brought into this rhythmical game!

Four-element games

It would be interesting to know what happens if we base our cycles on a different number of elements. Five is not a magic number; we could try playing the game with the number four; Let us therefore just take do-re-mi-fa and leave out the last note, sol. We do not have to do this, of course, we could leave out a middle note if we wanted the tunes to be more interesting. Or, better still, instead of do-re-mi-fa-sol, during the whole of the preceding exercises, we could have taken the black notes, as was indeed suggested in one example. If the dancers are musically fairly competent, they will be able to sing the black notes and they will find that much more pleasant-sounding tunes arise out of the exercises already given. The black notes generate a pentatonic scale, which gives a kind of a 'folk-tunish' flavour to the exercises. The tunes could be accompanied by the guitar and candlelight and quite an atmosphere could be created for an evening's entertainment, the dances being presented as 'mathematical folk-dances'.

So, let us get to work with our four notes. For the sake of argument, let us just take do-re-mi-fa. Let us see what happens if we take three of these:

do-re-mi / fa-mi-re.

We are back again at the beginning, after two bars. This suggests that after a six note bar, we shall be back after one go. The bars will repeat with monotonous regularity like a record gone wrong:

do-re-mi-fa-mi-re / do-re-mi-fa-mi-re.

So, we have found a six cycle. We can start superimposing other cycles on this six-cycle. Naturally, there having been one factor in common between three and six, we have a two-bar situation.

But now, let us take two or four in a bar. With four in a bar we have:

do-re-mi-fa / mi-re-do-re / mi-fa-mi-re

do-re-mi-fa / mi-re-do-re / mi-fa-mi-re

and we are back at the beginning after three bars. How come? This does not seem to be the same situation as before. Naturally, we now have to do with a six cycle, whereas before we had to do with an eight cycle. The reader is again invited to make guesses about how these cycles are likely to combine. He would probably guess that three has something to do with six and so has two. Since six is two times three, it is likely that we are now going to have to do with twos and threes, instead of twos and fours and eights which occurred in our games with the eight cycles. We might also be wondering whether we are going to have six-cycles as well? How could we get a six-cycle? It is fairly obvious that we should get a three-cycle by taking two notes in a bar instead of four in a bar; the sequence of bars

do-re / mi-fa / mi-re

will bring us back to the beginning in the same way as the sequence

do-re-mi-fa / mi-re-do-re / mi-fa-mi-re

will do. So, two in a bar, four in a bar, do not give us six-cycles; they give us three-cycles.

How is it possible to get a six-cycle out of our do-re-mi-fa-mi-re cycle? It was possible to get an eight-cycle out of the do-re-mi-fa-sol-fa-mi-re cycle, so why not try? We have not tried a five-note bar yet. This is not very popular in music; I have not heard of a fifth of a note being used in musical notation but that may be just because I am not overly familiar with modern music. Hopefully, this will be introduced. So, let us take a fifth as a 'value' for each note and have a rhythm of five fifths. That will give us:

do-re-mi-fa-mi / re-do-re-mi-fa / mi-re-do-re-mi / fa-mi-re-do-re / mi-fa-mi-re-do / re-mi-fa-mi-re and then we are back to do-re-mi-fa-mi.

We have found a cycle of six bars. Clearly, in the same way, if we simply take one note, a long note for each bar,

/ do / re / mi / fa / mi / re /,

after six, we are back to the beginning, i.e. to do.

So, one note in the bar, and five notes in the bar, will bring back to the beginning of our cycle after six bars. Two notes in the bar, or four notes in the bar, will bring us back after three bars in the cycle, and three notes in the bar will bring us back after two bars; six notes in the bar will bring us back after one bar.

We could play the rhythm game differently by taking one arm to represent the position of the note in the 'bar' and the other arm would follow the up and down movements along our four-note scale.

The side that showed the position in the bar would vary as follows:

Figure 49

and so on. The arm that went 'up and down the scale' would move as follows:

Figure 50

and so on. The latter would give us a six-cycle on which we could superimpose the four-cycle determined by the other arm.

Figure 51

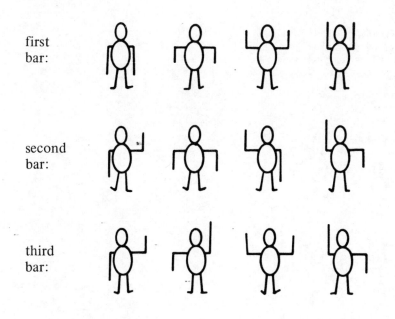

first
bar:

second
bar:

third
bar:

Reversals

Now, so far, we have been using only one type of way of complicating either a six beat or an eight rhythm in superimposing other rhythmes on them. Each time, we have followed the same rule, that is of just going on to the next part of the cycle. In our four element games consisting of do-re-mi-fa, we have a six-bar cycle, because

do-re-mi-fa-mi-re / do-re-mi-fa-mi-re

is really a six-beat rhythm, between beginnings of the same pattern. When we go through the cycle,

do-re-mi-fa / mi-re-do-re / mi-fa-mi-re and back to do-re-mi-fa

again, this means that we simply follow the same rule all the time as we go on to the next bar.

We could make matters more complex. Instead of going on to the next bar of a cycle, we could reverse the bar we have just done. If we are singing the notes, this might be a bit difficult, but if we are producing the notes by arm movement or foot movement, that is displacement of the body, it will be much easier to carry out a reversal. For example, here is a sequence of a mixture of 'goings on' and 'reversals'. Let us start again with our four notes, do-re-mi-fa, and do a going on, then a reversal and so on. This is how it goes:

Figure 52

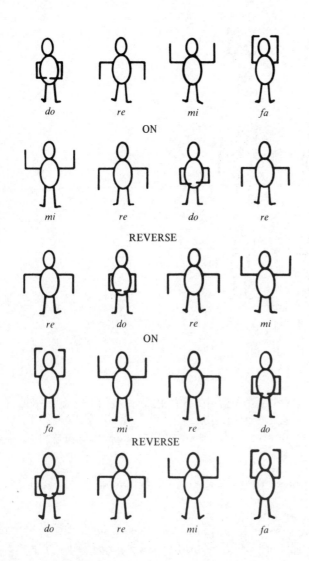

and we are back to where we started. So, we see that by going on, reversing, going on, reversing, we come back to the original position. Equally, going on, and then going on, and then going on, we come back to the original position. Equally obviously, if we reverse and then we reverse, we get back to the original position.

The reader might already be wondering if he has seen this kind of thing before; he did, in the first chapter. We have reproduced the three-cornered waltz situation. To make the situation more fun, we could have the three-cornered waltz danced on one side of the room and the rhythm exercise done on the other side of the room. One could be the signal for the other. The only difficulty is that the actions in the rhythm exercise are the 'states' of the game and it is these 'states' that we change by the *ON* and the *REVERSE* (the operators in this game), whereas in the dance, the *positions* of the dancers are the states of the game and the *movements* are the

56

operators by means of which we obtain new sets of positions for the dancers, starting from given ones.

We would have to agree that for each possible bar in the rhythm game, there would have to be a still position of the three-cornered waltz and that every time we said GO ON, the waltzers would take a left step, for example, and every time the rhythm command was REVERSE, they would take a boy's twiddle, or some such, in the three-cornered waltz. They would find that the corresponding situations would always arise regularly with the correctly determined corresponding bars in the rhythm game. Here is an exercise of this kind, described diagrammatically, as performed on the one hand by three waltzers and on the other hand by somebody running up and down on the do-re-mi-fa scale.

It will be seen that the sequence of 'operators':

LEFT, TWIDDLE, LEFT, TWIDDLE,

as well as:

GO ON, REVERSE, GO ON, REVERSE

brings us back to the initial position of each game.

Figure 53

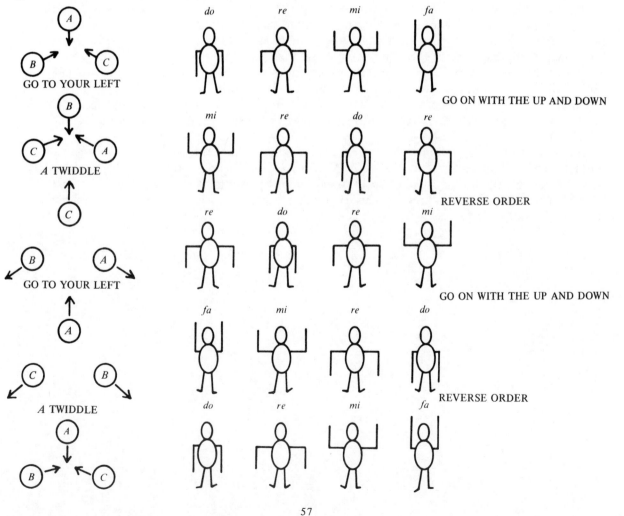

Somebody might be wondering, by now, whether the dihedral eightsome reel could be imitated by means of some rhythmical exercise. Naturally, all he has to do is to bring in the fifth note and, of course, he will have to make sure that the initial position is reached after four bars. This is because a left move has to be done four times to bring us back to the initial position in the dihedral square-dance reel, whereas we only needed three left moves to achieve this in the case of the three-cornered waltz.

Now, we know that a six-note bar will have the property required. It remains to be seen whether an ON followed by a REVERSE followed by an ON followed by a REVERSE, will still bring us back to the same bar in the rhythmical game in the same way as LEFT followed by a PARTNERS CHANGE OVER followed by a LEFT followed by a PARTNERS CHANGE OVER, brings the dancers in the foursome or eightsome dance back to the original position. This can easily be verified as follows: Suppose we start with do-re-mi-fa-sol-fa. Let us say we go ON. Then we have: mi-re-do-re-mi-fa. Now let us do the REVERSE which gives us fa-mi-re-do-re-mi. Now let us go ON which gives us fa-sol-fa-mi-re-do. Now, finally, let us REVERSE and we get do-re-mi-fa-sol-fa which is where we started.

Clearly, these games are really different versions of each other, from the point of view of the kind of things that can follow each other in succession. It is only the actual steps or moves that are different. The events in the dances are to do with each other in the same way as the events in the rhythmical games are to do with each other. We say, in mathematics, that the two games possess the same structure. The elements of the game hang together in the same way, and this is how one is really an image of the other. We are really playing the *same game* from the point of view of events hanging together. We merely fill up the 'structure' with different contents and so obtain different games, but ones which are different only in content but not in 'hanging togetherness'. So, the four-cornered reel is a different dance from the five note rhythmical game, but the way the moves in it are to do with each other, is the same in one game as it is in the other game.

The process of realizing that two different sets of content have the same *structure* is a crucial mental event in the all-important process of ABSTRACTION. In the modern world a great many new and very abstract ideas are constantly forced on us by events. It is only those of us who have learned to flex our 'thinking muscles' that will come out on top in this confusing and ever-increasing variety of newness.

4. Tactile games

How to make a tactile game out of a movement game

IN THE LAST three chapters, we have been exploring ways in which people, or in particular children can come to grips with mathematical ideas using their bodies. We used the movement of the body itself, from place to place, and we used the movement of the arms and legs, as well. We have not yet got down to small movements such as the movements of fingers. On the whole, we use our fingers for touching and feeling, to see what objects are like and becoming familiar with that aspect of the world which we can explore by means of direct bodily contact. In the previous chapters, we have been exploring ways in which we can discover things about the world, through moving about in it or through moving our own body from one position to another.

In this chapter, we shall be concerned with the sense of touch. Since the sense of touch is mostly experienced through fingers, we shall be dealing mostly with either finger exercises or simply with exercises of moving objects, from place to place that are distinguishable by the sense of touch from one another. The exercises in this chapter should, therefore, be able to be performed by blind people as well.

It is not hard to see that we can perform the rhythm games with our five fingers. All we have to do is to start with the thumb on our right hand and touch a surface with it. This is followed by the index, then the middle, then the ring and then the little finger. Then we go back to the ring, to the middle, to the index finger and to the thumb and so on. In other words, we can run up and down a 'five finger scale' much as we do in finger exercises on the piano, except that in a five finger exercise we have no need to cross fingers over, in the way we need to do when we play the scales on the piano.

It is also possible to represent the five elements of a five-element scale by means of objects having different shapes. For example, we can take a ball, a cylinder, a cube, a triangular prism and, say, a flat rectangular block. These five can easily be distinguished by touch from one another, even with the eyes closed. We may put them in certain particular positions, say on five places along a semi-circle or along a straight line and play the games in this way.

Counting and adding games

There are many interesting games to be played with our fingers which are of an arithmetical character. In fact fingers have been used for counting as far back as recorded history reaches. Witness also the priority given to ten (in our own system) and to five and ten (V, X, L, C in the Roman system). Quite young children will be ready to play with their parents at home or with their kindergarten or grade teacher at school. We might decide to give certain numerical values to our different fingers. For instance, we could say that the thumb is worth *one* and that the index finger is worth *two. One* could be represented by a single pebble or by a shell or by any other single object that we can find. Objects such as beer bottle tops will do, or any other objects of which we can find quite a few.

So, if the thumb is put out, that means one bottle top needs to be put out.

If the index finger is put out, that means two.

If both of them are put out, clearly, we are showing one together with two, since we are showing a thumb together with an index finger. This will indicate three.

In order to show four, we need another finger, so showing the middle finger could in this game mean four.

The middle finger with the thumb will mean *five.*

The middle finger with the index finger will mean *six.*

The middle, the index and the thumb will mean *seven.*

Now we have tried all the possible ways in which we can use our thumb; our index finger and our middle finger. We must go on to our ring finger, which will be worth *eight,* this being the next number. In this way, we can count up to 31 with the fingers of one hand. It goes like this:

		Little	Ring	Middle	Index	Thumb
1	thumb					1
2	index				1	0
3	index-thumb				1	1
4	middle			1	0	0
5	middle-thumb			1	0	1
6	middle-index			1	1	0
7	middle-index-thumb			1	1	1
8	ring		1	0	0	0
9	ring-thumb		1	0	0	1
10	ring-index		1	0	1	0
11	ring-index-thumb		1	0	1	1
12	ring-middle		1	1	0	0
13	ring-middle-thumb		1	1	0	1
14	ring-middle-index		1	1	1	0
15	ring-middle-index-thumb		1	1	1	1
16	little	1	0	0	0	0
17	little-thumb	1	0	0	0	1
18	little-index	1	0	0	1	0
19	little-index-thumb	1	0	0	1	1
20	little-middle	1	0	1	0	0
21	little-middle-thumb	1	0	1	0	1
22	little-middle-index	1	0	1	1	0

	Little	Ring	Middle	Index	Thumb
23 little-middle-index-thumb	1	0	1	1	1
24 little-ring	1	1	0	0	0
25 little-ring-thumb	1	1	0	0	1
26 little-ring-index	1	1	0	1	0
27 little-ring-index-thumb	1	1	0	1	1
28 little-ring-middle	1	1	1	0	0
29 little-ring-middle-thumb	1	1	1	0	1
30 little-ring-middle-index	1	1	1	1	0
31 little-ring-middle-index-thumb	1	1	1	1	1

and so we have reached 31. Any number under 32 can thus be represented by touching the surface of something such as the table at which we might be sitting, with a certain number of fingers or simply by showing them to someone else (if we wish to see what we are doing as well as feel it).

The regularities in the above table are sufficiently striking not to require any further 'explanations'.

Adding games could now be played, using fingers. We can show any number we choose with the fingers of the right hand and another number with those of the left hand. It is best, in the beginning, not to use the little finger, that is to choose numbers under 16. In this way when we add them, the sum can still be represented on the fingers of one hand. It will be realized very shortly that if we have two thumbs showing, they are together worth one index finger and if we have two index fingers showing in an addition sum, they will be worth one middle finger and if there are two middle fingers showing, they will be worth one ring finger. So, we can have, for example, the following addition:

		R	M	I	T
13 + 15 = ?					
13 will be ring-middle-thumb	or	1	1	0	1
15 will be ring-middle-index-thumb	or	1	1	1	1

If we add these up, two thumbs together will give us one index. So, there will be no thumb in the final sum. There is already one index and so with the other index there will be two indices. That will give us one middle finger altogether. Since we already have two middle fingers, with the middle finger we just obtained out of two index fingers, we will have three middle fingers. That leaves really one middle only, since two of the middles will be equivalent to one ring. That gives us three rings altogether. Two of these ring fingers will be equivalent to a little finger and and one ring will remain so the answer will be: little-ring-middle. We can easily verify that this is 16 + 8 + 4, namely 28, of course

15 + 13 = 28

It is *not recommended* that this kind of game should be used as a *quick method* of adding 13 to 15, but it is an interesting *mental exercise* to split numbers into sums of powers of 2. Each finger has a value which is a power of 2. The thumb is the 0th power, the index is the first power, the middle the second power, the ring the third power and the little finger the fourth power, that is 1, 2, 4, 8 and 16 respectively. Any number up to and including 31 can be expressed as a sum of such powers and we never need to take any of them more than once. In other words, we do not ever need the same power twice. This is fairly obvious, since if we have a certain power of 2 twice, we clearly have the next power, so we cannot have had it twice, if we take the most economical number of terms, consisting of 1, 2, 4, 8 or 16 to add up to our particular number. The mathematical reader will realize immediately that what we are doing is working in what is known as base 2.

It is very easy to further generalize this game into counting in base 3. All we need to do is to use *both our hands simultaneously*. The thumb on one hand or on the other would mean *one*. If we use the thumbs to touch the table, that means *two* and so the index finger will now mean *three*. To *four* will be one index and one thumb, five will be one index add two thumbs. When we come to *six* we need two index fingers, *seven* will be two index fingers and one thumb, *eight* will be two index fingers and two thumbs and then we have run out of fingers so we have to get on to the next finger which is the middle finger. So in this game, the middle finger will have the value of *nine*. It will already be seen that we are now using the powers of three for the values of our fingers, whereas we were using the powers of two for these values in the previous game. Clearly, if we use the two middle fingers, two index fingers and two thumbs, we obtain 26. The ring finger is the next one to use, after having run out of fingers. Therefore, the ring finger will have to represent 27. If we add the values of two rings, two middles, two index fingers and two thumbs, we shall get exactly 80 and so the little finger will represent 81. By showing all the fingers we will get 242, which is one less than 243, the latter being the fifth power of three. This kind of game can already lead to quite complex and interesting exercises of practical value in the school room as well as for children's homework or Saturday afternoon amusement on the beach or in the backyard.

Naturally, *adding games* can be developed out of this situation as well. We shall need to have one person to show the first number and another person to show the second number and the third person has to compute the sum. In this case, three thumbs are worth an index, three index fingers a middle, three middle fingers a ring and three ring fingers a little finger. If we want to go beyond 242, we can use toes or we can use other artificial objects for representing fingers.

Another way of playing this game would be to tie with a bit of ribbon on each finger showing its own value. This can be done by sticking a piece of paper on the ribbon showing the value in ordinary numerals or else showing the same value by drawing a lot of dots. Of course, drawing 81 dots is not going to be very helpful because unless we know that there are 81 dots there, we are not going to spend a lot of time counting them. So, maybe simply writing down in numerals, or in words, the value of each finger, would be sufficient. It is not necessary to transform these numerals into ordinary 'base ten' numerals in the addition problems. In other words, we do not need 'tens and units'. It will be quite sufficient to consider numbers as made up of so many ones and so many threes and so many nines and so many 27's and so many 81's and so on.

10110

111

Instead of fingers
here individual children
are used for "counting"
and "adding"

1111

63

Take for example the following exercise:

Figure 54

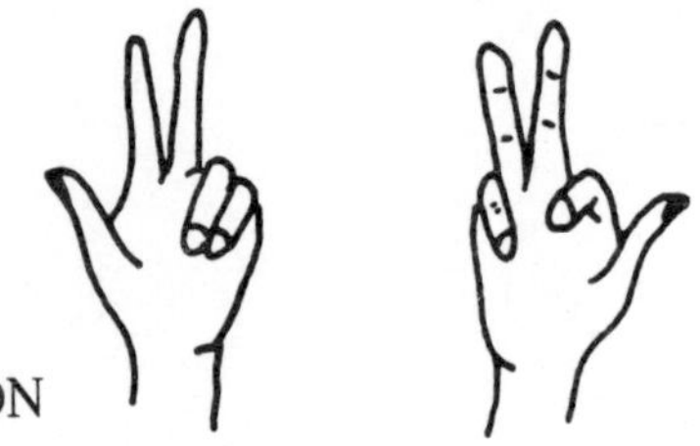

FIRST
PERSON

L	(27's)	(9's)	(3's)	(1's)
R		M	I	T
I		2	1	2

SECOND
PERSON

L	(27's)	(9's)	(3's)	(1's)
R		M	I	T
		1	1	1

There are three thumbs, these are worth one index.
There are two index fingers, and with the one that comes out of three thumbs, we have three index fingers.
    So all the index and thumbs shown are worth just one middle finger.
    There are three middle fingers, these are worth one ring finger.

    With the one ring finger already there, we have altogether
        2 ring fingers, 1 middle finger
    i.e. 2×27 + 1×9 = 63.
The first person's number was
    $1 \times 27 + 2 \times 9 + 1 \times 3 \times 2 \times 1$ = 50.
The second person's number was
    $1 \times 9 + 1 \times 3 + 1 \times 1$ = 13.

Some rhythms turned into touch. Games with squares

We shall now see how we can play the rhythmical and the dance games by the use of touch. For example, we could cut out a cardboard square, such as shown on Figure 55, with a circle in one corner, a triangle in another, a star in another and a square in another. We can hold the square upright in a vertical plane, holding the two lower corners with our left and right hands, respectively. In the figure, we see that when the left hand holds the square and the right hand holds the star, then the square can be said to be in the square-star position. It will easily be seen that we can hold it upright in this way in eight different positions. These are:

64

Figure 55

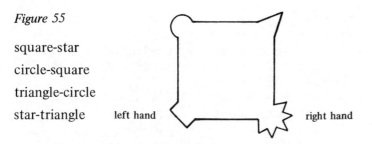

square-star

circle-square

triangle-circle

star-triangle   left hand   right hand

or we could change left hands and right hands, that is we could turn the square over to show the opposite face of it and have:

   star-square   square-circle   circle-triangle   and   triangle-star.

In order to move our cardboard square from one of its positions to any other, it is enough to consider two moves. One, for example, is to turn it round in the clockwise sense. This will turn it from square-star into star-triangle; it will turn from star-triangle into triangle-circle and from triangle-circle into circle-square and from circle-square into square-star. In other words, four successive clockwise turns will bring the square back into its original position. Naturally, we could have taken the counter-clockwise turn and then we would have gone through the positions on the same side of the square but in the opposite order. Of course, we could simply take the shapes in the opposite hands which would be a kind of a reversal move, which would change a square-star into a star-square. At the start we are holding the square in the left hand and the star in the right and when we can change hands we are holding the star with the left hand and the square with the right. It will probably he seen that this will correspond to one of the twiddling moves in the dance game and to the reversal move in the rhythmical games. The 'turning round' will correspond to the going-on move, in the rhythmical games, the going to your left or going to your right in the dance game.

   Are the 'internal rules' or 'connections' the same in this game as in the other like games? We can verify, for example, that if we start from the position square-star and we take a clockwise move, then a reversal move then a clockwise move and then a reversal move, we return to the square-star position. In other words, the abstract properties which we have already extracted from the other game can also be verified for this one. In fact, we could use our square as a kind of command for the dancers to carry out certain steps in the dance game or for doing certain operations in the rhythm games. Conversely, the rhythmical or singing games could be played which could serve as instructions for the person who is holding the square and he would have to follow with his square what the rhythm people were doing. To each of the positions chosen would, of course, correspond, one of the eight bars that we can find in the rhythmical game in which there are four cycles of bars in one direction and four cycles in the reverse direction.

   There is no need to go to the trouble of cutting out a whole square with the corners 'frilled' with our four shapes. We can just take four shapes: a circle, a triangle, a star and a square or any other objects easily distinguishable from each other and simply put them down in a row. We could decide on the following 'moves'.

   (a)   Pick up the end shape, the square in this case, and put it in the front. That means that from the sequence circle-triangle-star-square, we would obtain the sequence square-circle-triangle-star. If we put the end one in the front now, we would now get star-square-circle-triangle and if we put the triangle in front now, we would get triangle-star-square-circle and if we put the circle in front now we would have circle-triangle-star-square. In other words, putting the end one in the front of the row, which we might call the 'last shall be first' move, will generate a *cycle of four,* since we have four shapes to go through.

(b)   What would be the reversal move in this case? There are several possible reversal moves. For example, we might change the middle two as well as the end two at the same time, that is if we start with circle-triangle-star-square, we could finish up with square-star-triangle-circle. That means, in effect, that we will have changed the order and the last will be the first, the first will be the last, the third will be the second and the second will be the third.

This last move will correspond exactly to the reversal of the notes in the rhythmical game. So, it is hardly surprising that this move will behave in the same way in connection with the 'last shall be first' as the move did in the square dances we have been played up to now.

Let us see what happens if we change the first two with each other, and at the same time we change the last two with each other. Let us combine it with the 'last shall be first' move. Start with:
   circle-triangle-star-square.
Change the first pair, change the second pair,
   triangle-circle-square-star.
'Last shall be first'
   star-triangle-circle-square.
Change the first pair and change the last pair
   triangle-star-square-circle.
'Last shall be first'
   circle-triangle-star-square.
In other words, this changing rule has the same properties as the reversal move in relation to the four cycle.

But we could get even more 'radical' and still find the same connections. Let us take, for example, a change of the first shape with the third shape but without changing the second shape with the fourth. In other words, the first shape will go where the third shape now is and the third shape will go where the first shape now is, we will leave the second one where it is and we will leave the fourth one where it is. Let us see if this move combines with the 'last shall be first' move following the same connections as did the reversal rule.

We start again with circle-triangle-star-square.
Change the first with the third,
   star-triangle-circle-square.
'Last shall be first'
   square-star-triangle-circle
Change the first with the third
   triangle-star-square-circle
'Last shall be first'
   circle-triangle-star-square,
as we were in the beginning.

We might be tempted to believe that any kind of change of two or of four elements will do this trick. This is far from being so. Let us, for example, change the first with the second but without changing the third and the fourth, that is the first shape goes where the second was, the second goes where the first was, the third stays where it is and the fourth stays where it is. Let us call this 'first pair change'.

Start again with circle-triangle-star-square.
Change the first pair
   triangle-circle-star-square,

66

'Last shall be first'
   square-triangle-circle-star,
First pair change
   triangle-square-circle-star,
'Last shall be first'
   star-triangle-square-circle.

In other words, *we have not reached the initial stage.* So there are some exchanging rules which *do* and others *do not* follow the same pattern in connection with the 'last shall be first' and so there is something to find out.

Of course, if we look at the square shown on Figure 1, the reason for this discrepancy is easy to discover. It is possible to change the position of the first and the third vertex on the square without changing the second and the fourth. All we have to do is to hold the square at the corners which have the shapes which correspond to the second and the fourth positions in our present game and twiddle the square around a half turn so that the other two shapes change places. But, if we wish to change the two neighbouring shapes, we cannot do so without changing the other two neighbouring shapes, without, that is, breaking or twisting the square. So, a certain amount of geometry of the square is being learnt here in relation to the number of ways in which you can change things, that is in relation to the study of permutations.

It will not be difficult to see that there are 24 ways in which you can put down a circle, a triangle, a star and a square next to each other and yet there are only eight ways in which you can put a square down so as to occupy the same space. So, its corners can only be permuted in eight different ways whereas four arbitrary objects which are not tied together rigidly in any way can be permuted in 24 different ways. It will be an interesting exercise to draw the three different squares that we need in order to produce out of them all the 24 possible ways of permuting the four different objects. These three squares must be such that there is no way in which we can put one square on top of the other so that the corresponding shapes cover each other. If such complete covering were possible, our second square would not be, so to speak, a 'new' square and consequently would not produce new permutations of the corners.

It will be interesting to inquire, for example, that if we give ourselves two of these moves – for example, last shall be first as one and first and third change places with each other – how many of these moves will be required and in what order, to get from any possible position to any other position? It will be found that never more than three moves are necessary if the right ones are chosen and if they are carried out in the right order. Games could be played of a competitive nature in challenging people to get from certain positions to certain other positions. We could make a little cardboard regular octahedron on the faces of which all the eight possible positions of the square are drawn. The octahedron can be used as a die which is thrown and the task is given to the opposing player to reach the position required in the least number of moves. The number of moves is noted and the player then becomes the die thrower, the first die thrower becomes the player and he has to solve the problem of reaching the permutation shown on the octahedron in the least number of moves. Each player gets a point for each move he has to make and, clearly, the player with the least number of points will win the game. Naturally, sometimes, it is possible to go from an arrangement to another arrangement in one move, sometimes you need two and in a few cases, you need three moves. For any given starting position, there are just two for which three moves are required, there are three for which two moves are required, there are two for which only one move is required and there is one for which no move is required, namely if we are there already.

Tetrahedron or 'tent' games: triangles

We could complicate the four-shape game a little further by allowing other kinds of transformations which have, perhaps nothing to do with the square. We might consider cyclic transformations in which one particular position is unaltered. For example, we might say the first position is unaltered and the others can be moved in a cyclic order. For instance, the second shape goes to where the third was and the third to where the fourth was and the fourth to where the second was, and the first one stays put. Or, we may say that the third shape stays put and the first goes where the fourth was, the fourth goes where the second was and the second where the first was and so on. It will be found that we can reach all possible, reachable positions, in not more than four goes. Naturally, we shall have to have some way of determining which the reachable positions are. All the 24 cannot be reached in this way as can be verified by trying. It will be found that only 12 of them can be reached by these transformations in which, three shapes take a cyclic change. In other words, our harvest of positions is slightly richer than if we imitate the square but not as good as going the whole hog and getting all the 24 possible permutations. Now, to imitate this by a geometrical figure, we would need to make a tetrahedron.

This is very easily made; cut out an equilateral triangle out of cardboard, mark the mid-points of the sides, join these mid-points by straight lines and bend the cardboard at these points, leaving the middle triangle horizontal and the other three-triangles so-formed, can be closed together rather like the petals of a flower which close in the evening. All we need now is some adhesive tape. to fix the closure.

Having constructed the tetrahedron, we shall soon see that it has four corners in the same way as a square has four corners. But the square only has two faces whereas the tetrahedron has four. So, we have something more in the tetrahedron than we have in the square. We can find four objects left-over from Christmas decorations. Say a marble, a small cube, perhaps a pyramid and a star. We can glue the marble on one corner, the cube on the other corner, the pyramid on another corner and the star on the remaining corner. There is no need to have just these shapes; any other four shapes that are easily distinguishable from one another will do. Now, we can place the tetrahedron so made in front of us. There will be a shape at the upper corner or vertex and let us place it so that there is a corner nearest to us. We can read the position of the tetrahedron by looking at the shape at the top and the shape at the bottom nearest to us. If, for instance, there is a cube at the top and a star at the position nearest to us, then we shall say that the tetrahedron is in the cube-star position. Let us say, that in this case, on our left, is the pyramid

Figure 56

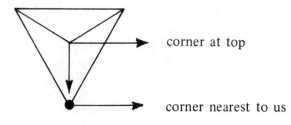

corner at top

corner nearest to us

and on our right is the marble. Then, we could say, for example, that this position is associated to cube-star-pyramid-marble or to liken it to our previous game, square-star-triangle-circle. This was one of the 'reachable' positions obtained by reversal from the initial position circle-triangle-star-square. However we move the tetrahedron, as long as we put it back with one of its vertices nearest to us, we shall get one of the positions which is obtainable by one of these three cycles which we have just described, applied to the initial position with which we began.

We can then take a dodecahedron which can be purchased in bookstores or paper shops as calendars where for each month there is a pentagon with the dates and the days indicated for the year and stick upon each of these twelve faces, one of the permutations obtainable by throwing the tetrahedron around. We will see that there are just 12 of these. Then we can play the tetrahedron game with the dodecahedron dice in the same way as we played the square game with the octahedron dice.

It will not take long for the reader to guess that the three-cornered waltz can be realized, for example, by means of an equilateral triangle in the form of a game using touch. Let us take an equilateral triangle and in one corner stick a circle, in another a square, and in another a star. So, let us hold one corner with the left hand and the other corner with the right hand. There will be the third corner which is held up above the other two corners. In that case, if the left hand corner has the square and the right hand corner the star, then we shall call this position square-star. We can use a rotation of the equilateral triangle in its own plane, say in the clockwise direction; then from square-star, we shall get in star-circle and from star-circle we shall get to circle-square and from circle-square back to square-star. We can also change hands and what was held in the left hand can be taken by the right hand and what was taken by the right can be taken be the left. In this way, for example, a square-star position is changed for a star-square position.

We can verify that the clockwise turn has to be repeated three times to regain the original position, the reversal obviously has to be repeated twice to regain it and then if we combine clockwise turns and reversals, we will have to have a clockwise turn followed by a reversal, followed by a clockwise turn, followed by a reversal, as always, to reach the original position.

The 'same' game can be played with three objects, using any kinds of permutations and it will be seen that if we try to change the order of a circle, a square and a star put out in the row, in any way whatsoever, we can reproduce this order by means of putting the equilateral triangle down in a certain way. For example, the upper corner could correspond to the middle one in the row, the left hand corner to the left hand one in the row and the right hand corner of the triangle to the one at the right hand end of the row. In other words, there are six possible permutations of three objects and there are six possible positions for the cardboard model of the equilateral triangle in which it will occupy the same space on the table. So, in the same way as before, we could use the turning and twiddling of such a model as an equilateral triangle as a command for the dancers to carry out their moves.

In this chapter we have used *positions in space* to which we have referred the moves. We have not connected the moves to the shapes themselves independently of the positions which they occupy. Obviously, we could have done it the other way round as well. For instance, in the four-shape permutation game, instead of saying that the shapes occupying the first and the third positions have to be changed over, we should say that any two particular shapes must be changed over. For instance, we might say that the circle and the star must be changed over. But, in this case, we must be careful that the last shall be first rule, needs to be expressed in terms of which shape takes the place of which other shape. For example, instead of saying that the last shall be the first, we will have to say that the square takes the place of the circle and the circle takes the place of the triangle, the triangle takes the place of the star and the star takes the place of the square. If we keep to the same way of expressing the moves, we shall not get into any trouble. The triangle can be made out of circular coasters found in saloons and these can be put together to make a triangular shape, stuck together with sello-tape as long as the same print is clearly visible on each side of the mat. A sort of tetrahedron shape can also be made by putting one coaster on the table and three others, sloping towards each other as a kind of three-cornered roof on top. There will be a hole at the top instead of the vertex as in the case of a 'proper' model of a tetrahedron. But, again, the position of the four-coaster tent-shaped object can be determined by the designs on the two coasters that are facing you. You need to make sure that one join of two sloping mats is put close to yourself. Then the left one followed by the right one, in relation to yourself, will give you the position of the 'tetrahedron'.

As we shall see in the next chapter, beer coasters are very good material for making other, but possibly more visual, types of representations of the games we have been considering.

How to reach all permutations of four objects

To reach the 24 possible permutations, we can take, for example, four different coloured knitting needles or chop-sticks and put them together at the middle, sticking them with adhesive tape or plasticine, but in such a way that a square is made when we are looking down at the extremities of the knitting needles, as well as when we are looking at them sideways. This, in practice, is a little difficult to make. When we have succeeded, we can look at the structure from above and enumerate the colours, say from one particular corner in a clockwise sense. It will be seen that all the 24 possible permutations of colours can be realized by putting this construction down in different ways. There are six possible squares — looking at it from above, looking at it from below, from the front, from the back, from the right and from the left. Each position can be arranged in four possible ways since we can turn the structure round by one quarter turn along, whichever way we are looking at it.

If the needle job appears too complicated, all we have to do is take a dice and some coloured magic markers and make one corner red and the opposite corner to that along the principal diagonal the same colour red. Then we choose another corner which we might call blue and the opposite corner to that will also be blue, and any remaining corner we can call yellow, and the opposite corner to that will also be yellow, then there will be only tow corners left which will be green. In this way, the knitting needles or chop-sticks will be replaced by the principal diagonals of the cube. In either case, we can place our four-coloured construction in any one of the 24 ways. We can then play a much more complex game with the 24 permutations and all the possible positions of the cube. The mathematics of this is somewhat complex and it is not recommended that the beginner should start immediately exploring all the possibilities of the 24 permutations and how the changes of position of the four shapes correspond to the various ways in which we can spin the cube about its 13 different possible axes of rotation. Naturally, any reader who will regard this as a challenge can solve the problem from first principles, simply by using his grey matter. In fact it will be easier to do so than to wade through the usual abstruse 'explanations' to be found in mathematical text-books.

It is possible to introduce other tactile experiences, not merely the touching of a table with fingers or the touching of certain shapes with the fingers. We could associate certain elements of a game with certain tactile sensations on the hand. For example, we might take the four fingers, starting with index, middle, ring and little finger, and touch the end of the fingers, the middle of the fingers, or the base of the fingers. That would give us twelve different ways in which we can associate the elements of a game with tactile sensations. If we wish twenty-four instead of twelve, we could touch the palm or not do so. Let us not forget that one person has to *give* the sensation and the other person has to experience it, so the giver of the signal will use, for instance, his thumb and his index finger for passing on the sensation, so the thumb will touch the palm or not and the index finger will touch some part of the finger of the subject. We can have the finger contacts with or without the thumb touching palm. This gives us 24 different sensations. These sensations can be associated, for example, to different shapes of different sizes or of different thicknesses, or to different positions of the arms and legs in the bodily movement games. We could have the following 24 'tactile sensation' elements in correspondence with 'bodily position'.

Elements are as shown on the accompanying diagram.

Figure 57

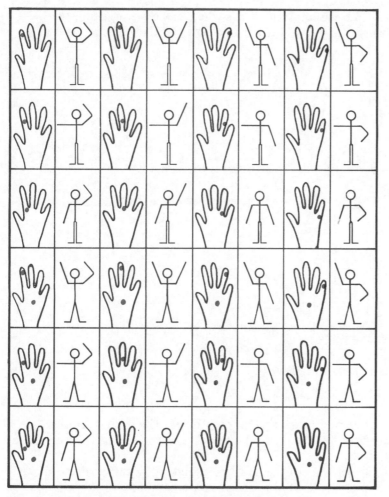

The dots show where the touch-sensations occur.

71

The four fingers could correspond to the positions of the right arm. The part of the finger that is touched could correspond to positions of the left arm. Whether the palm is touched or not could correspond to, say, having your legs astride or having them together, so, say, the left arm up could correspond to having the tip of your finger touched, the left arm horizontal could correspond to having the middle of your finger touched, and the left arm down could correspond to the base of your finger being touched. Further, the index finger in the touching game could correspond to having your right arm over your head, the middle finger could correspond to having your arm horizontal up to the elbow and the rest vertically up. The ring finger could correspond to your right arm horizontal up to the elbow and the rest vertically down, and the little finger being touched could correspond to the arm vertically down to the elbow and the remainder of the arm horizontal placed across the front of the body.

In this case any game we play with the right and the left arms, and the legs being astride or together, can be transferred to a corresponding game which is played by means of the sense of touch. For example, we might leave out the horizontal position of the left arm; also, we would leave out the middle part of the finger being touched. We might also disregard the palm being touched by the thumb. In this case, instead of 24, only eight positions would be left. We could say that we have a cyclic move which will move upwards when the left arm is pointing upwards, and will move downwards when the left arm is hanging down in the vertical position.

Figure 58

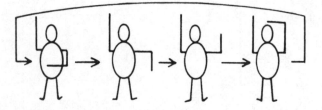

upward movement of right arm with left arm up.

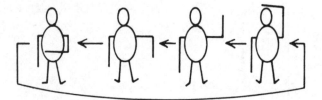

downward movement of right arm with left arm down.

It is left to the reader to play the corresponding game with the fingers. The fingers will be touched in one order when the tips are being touched and in the opposite order when the bases are touched.

In the arm-movement exercise this corresponds to the left arm up having an opposite cycle from the cycle we have with the left arm down. This in turn corresponds exactly to the way in which the dancers dance round clockwise, for example, when they are moving to the right but facing inwards, then dancing counterclockwise when they are going to the right but facing outwards. And so these movements, as well as the corresponding games on the scales can be played with the arms changing places as with the fingers being touched. A person can touch, of course, his own fingers, that is, touch his left hand with the fingers of his right hand and somebody else can then follow by means of a movement game or any other kind of game, such as the painting games, which we shall describe in the next chapter.

How to reach the 24 permutations of four objects A, B, C, D is left as one exercise for the reader. However here are some hints:

Figure 58a

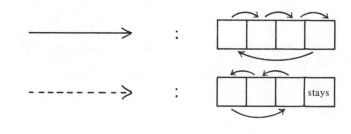

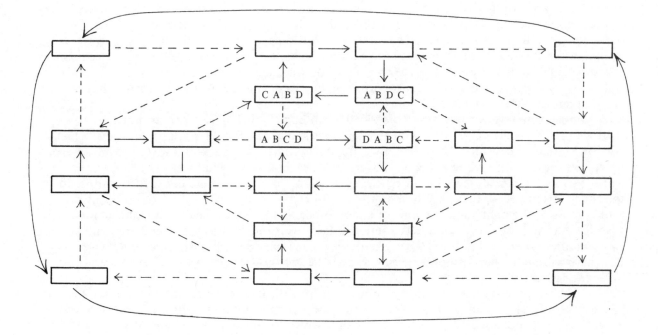

5. Visual games

Visual counting games

WE HAVE NOW TRACED different kinds of activities through the bodily movement complex and the tactile complex. Let us now go on to the sense modality of sight. We can draw, we can paint, and we can look, for example, although of course drawing and painting do use touch, as we need to hold a pencil or a paintbrush. But essentially this is in the service of sight as we are combining colours or we are putting shapes on paper in order to draw a picture or produce a painting.

Let us see how the counting game can be 'painted'. We can choose four different colours, for example, white, yellow, orange, and red and we can tell the children to draw some houses. We might decide that each house must have just one window, and the window can be white or yellow or orange or red. We may be imitating, for instance, the effect of the setting of the sun on windows of the house. First it's white, when the sun isn't directly shining on it. It becomes yellow when the sun's rays fall on it. It may be orange when the sun is near the horizon. And just before setting, when it reddens the whole sky, the window becomes red. So we could have a succession of sequences in time corresponding to certain acts or imaginary events of white, yellow, orange, and red. Any other sequence of colours corresponding to imaginary or real events that might occur in nature would do as well.

Of course, when we come to two windows the sunset story will have to be dropped, as we shall see in a moment. Let us start with two windows and make the restriction that the left-hand window can never be white. Accordingly we are able to have a yellow window on the left or an orange on the left, or a red window on the left. With each of these windows, we could have a white, yellow, orange, or red window on the right. Now we can put these in order according to the change from yellow to orange to red of the left-hand window followed by the changes in all four colours of the right-hand window, or in any other way in which we or our children may wish to order their houses. In any case there will be 12 possible houses that can be drawn with two windows. There will not be 16 because the left-hand window is not allowed to be white. But there will be four one-window houses, so together with these four we will have made 16 different houses.

Next we can proceed to three-window houses, again with the provision that we are not allowed to have the left-hand window white. So the left-hand window could be yellow or orange or red. To each of these possibilities there are 16 possible ways of colouring in the second and the third window because we are allowed to have a white for the second window; since all possible combinations are allowed for the second and the third window, we shall have 16 such combinations. So that makes 16 with a yellow left-hand window, 16 with an orange left-hand window and 16 with a red one. So we shall have 48 three window houses. The rule to be observed is never to have a white window with which to begin the row of windows. Added to the 16 we have already drawn, we now have 64 houses.

74

We can, of course, go on to four-window houses but this would be rather cumbersome because we would finish up with 256 houses altogether. Some children may want to do this. In fact, very often, such repetitious work which involves classifying and the joy of verifying what they think is going to happen is something that children like doing, and very often on a rainy Saturday afternoon, if you have your child occupied with painting 256 houses with different coloured windows, it might indeed be a godsend.

To see how the house and the colouring of the windows is to do with the counting games can be seen immediately by reducing the number of colours to three. Let us just take white, yellow, and red. There can only be three such houses with only one window. There can be only six others with two windows, because, of course we are not allowed a white one to start with. We can have only a yellow or a red to start with, and to each one of these there are three other possible windows on the right, giving us six houses to add to our original three, making nine altogether. Having made these nine houses, we can build three-window houses in which the first window in the row can be either yellow or red but not white. To each of these, there will be nine possible ways to colour the remaining second and third windows. This means that we can have two times nine, or a total of 18 possible three-windowed houses. So by the time we have finished all the houses with one, two, and three windows, we shall have reached 27 houses. In the case of three colours, the four-windowed houses will not present a formidable problem. The reader will have by now guessed that he will finish with 81 houses. And it is only the inclusion of five-windowed houses that will produce a very large number of houses to be painted, namely 243, this being the fifth power of three.

This painting game corresponds to the finger game played with two hands, where the thumb is worth one, the index finger three, the middle finger nine, and the ring finger is worth 27. The colour white corresponds to 'none'. It is difficult to show 'no finger' as we cannot touch anything with no fingers. But we might make some other gesture instead. Yellow will indicate that one of a certain kind of finger is touching. So, for instance, one red window in the house would mean two thumbs, but one red window followed by one white window would mean two index fingers and no thumbs.

Here is a table of the full relationship between the house painting game and the finger game:

Figure 59

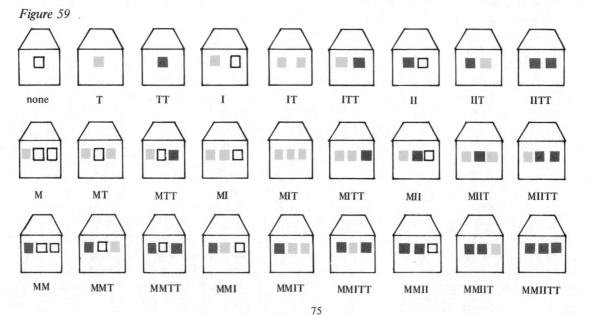

none	T	TT	I	IT	ITT	II	IIT	IITT
M	MT	MTT	MI	MIT	MITT	MII	MIIT	MIITT
MM	MMT	MMTT	MMI	MMIT	MMITT	MMII	MMIIT	MMIITT

Naturally there is no need to paint just houses. Flowers or trees or anything a child himself might fancy will do. There could be a white flower, a yellow flower, and an orange flower. The flowers will have to be arranged, of course, from left to right, or in some order because it is the positions of the flowers that count, in the same way as the positions of the windows determine where they will come in the sequence of houses or in the sequence of bunches of flowers.

Six-element visual games

It would be boring just to deal with the windows. Children will want to colour not just the windows of a house, but also its wall and its roof and possibly its chimney. So let us take, for example, three colours and let us colour three parts of the house each time. Children should be encouraged to draw different kinds of houses, not just the ordinary conventional house shown by an adult stereotype. Let them draw castles, little native huts, sky-scrapers, offices, any kind of buildings at all, and let their imaginations go. The only restriction is that in any one house all the windows should be of the same colour, all the doors should be of the same colour and the roof should have a certain determinate colour. If we use just three colours in every building, then having coloured the windows, doors and the roof, we could use any other colour for the chimney or any other parts of the house which could vary from house to house or could stay the same for all houses. For example, we could use red, blue, and yellow for the parts that we are considering as factors determining their 'kind' and green and orange and white or black or any other colours for the rest of the house that we are not considering as linked to the rules we are using. It will be seen that with three *relevant* colours, we can draw six different types. These would be the following:

Red wall,	blue windows	and yellow doors,
Red wall,	yellow windows	and blue doors,
Blue wall,	red windows	and yellow doors,
Blue wall,	yellow windows	and red doors,
Yellow wall,	red windows	and blue doors,
Yellow wall,	blue windows	and red doors.

We can see that we can make, for example, six parts of the town. In each part of town, the combinations of doors, windows, and walls ought to be the same. These would depict different districts. We could say that people, after a while, get tired of living in the same district, because they are always seeing red doors and blue walls and yellow windows and so they want a change. They might say that they do not like the windows being red or yellow or whatever they happen to be in their particular district and they would like the colour of the windows to be exchanged for the colour of the doors, but they are quite satisfied with the colour of the wall as it is. So then they go to another district where the walls are painted the same colour as in the old district, which pleases them, but the windows and the doors will be changed over. Of course if they get fed up with this again, but they still like the walls, they will just have to move back to their old district. But they might decide that now they like the colour of the windows in their new district but they would like to change the colour of the door with the colour of the wall, and the colour of the wall with the colour of the door. In that case they have to move to a corresponding district, and so on. Of course they might decide that they do not like anything the way it is, meaning that they would like, for instance, the colour of the door to become the colour of the window, the colour of the window to become the colour of the wall, and the colour of the wall to become the colour of the windows. Well, in this case, they would have to move to the corresponding district where this is so. Whatever the rule they think of for themselves, as long as it results in a situation where all three colours are used for the three parts of the buildings, they will find a district to which they can go. But if they say that the colour of the doors and of the windows needs to be the same as the colour of the wall, then they will not be able to find such a district because they have not built one. They will then have to build another town with different types of districts.

We can arrange the six districts in some regular way to have an overall architecture of the whole town. Here are some possible ways of doing this –

Figure 60

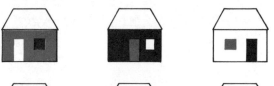

Figure 61

or

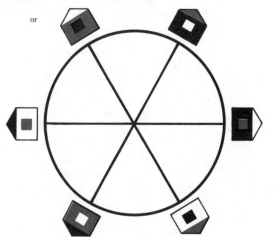

77

It will no doubt be already apparent to some that the moving game in the six-district town is really the same game as the three-cornered waltz. For example, turning right, that is, taking the place of the person on your right in the waltz could correspond to changing the colour of the door for the colour of the window, the colour of the window with the colour of the wall, and the colour of the wall for the colour of the door. And, for example, one of the twiddles could be represented by the colour of the window remaining unchanged, and the colours of the foor and the wall being replaced by one another. It will be seen that whichever part of the house we leave unchanged as long as we change over the colours of the other two parts we shall be doing something very akin to the twiddle moves. Any rule which changes all three colours will resemble the move of going to the place of the person on your right or else going to the place of the person on your left. In this way we now have a moving game, a touching game, and a seeing game for this kind of a structure or 'hanging-togetherness'. We shall also see later that the way in which the choreography of the dancing is arranged in different parts of the floor will lead to an interesting way of formulating the inner structure of these games through abstract types of *maps*. In a way a map of a town is abstract, since when we look at the streets, we are not looking at real streets. However, the *relationships* between the streets, such as parallelism, relative distance, and so on, are reproduced on the map. That is, we can foretell, by looking on the map of a town, what we are likely to come across as we walk or drive through the town. Naturally we must know how to *read the map*. For this reason it is good to have mathematical maps so that we can make predictions about what is likely to happen. Again, to do so requires some training in mathematical map-reading.

When we know what is going to happen, this knowledge can be expressed in the form of a *property of the map*. Such expressions will lend us to more mathematical ways of formulating properties. We shall then no longer speak just in terms of bodily movements or of touching fingers, or of painting houses, but in terms of *abstractions* which we shall have abstracted out of all these games.

Twelve-element visual games

Let us see what happens if we use four colours. We might choose red, blue, yellow, and green. We can colour the wall, the door, the windows, and the roof all differently, that is, every house should have the four colours in it. We shall see that there are 24 different ways of colouring our houses, and we are back at the '24 game'. If we wish to introduce the '12 game', we can say that from any particular colour scheme of a house, we can only paint another house by keeping one of the colours constant and changing all the other three. We shall find that if we do this we shall end up with 12 different kinds of house. This house colouring activity can be imitated by moving a tetrehedron around which has the four colours painted on its four corners. Each corner-position can be made to correspond to the doors, the wall, and the roof, respectively, as is shown in the diagram.

Figure 62

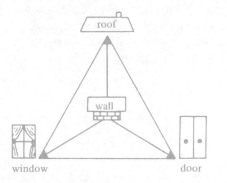

Each of the twelve positions of the tetrahedron will determine a way of colouring a house. Each time we wish to keep something unchanged, we hold still the corner of the tetrahedron associated with this part of the home, and twiddle the whole thing about this corner.

We could colour many other kinds of things. For example, let us dress a boy in many different ways, using four colours.

Figure 63

Exactly the same kinds of correspondence can be established between the equilateral triangle and the six districts in the town, or between the square and eight districts that we could then have in the town. In the latter case we would need to put down the square and decide, as shown on the diagram, to give an idea of which corner of the square represents which part of the house. For example the top left corner could be the roof, the top right corner the window, the bottom left corner the wall, and the bottom right corner the door, or this might be determined in any other way as long as we remain consistent with ourselves.

Figure 64

So by drawing and painting, we can introduce very similar mathematical ideas to those which we have already introduced by gymnastics, dancing, and rhythmics. It is left to the reader to discover how to organize 24 districts in the town, using just four colours.

What are points and lines?

We have not made use of one very important property of seeing. When we look at something, we look along the path of the rays of light that reach our eyes from the object seen. Since light travels along straight lines, the geometrical idea of the straight line could be introduced by noticing many different positions of objects being 'in line' with each other. This will enable us to play a number of different geometrical games and *prepare the ground for the abstractions of 'points' and of 'lines'.* The geometrical ideas of concurrence, collinearity, and other allied notions can be introduced as 'seeing games'.

Let us stand two people on a flat piece of ground not too close to each other, perhaps five or six feet away. Now let a third person walk around and stop as soon as he sees that one person is directly behind or in front of another person. The person who has just stopped walking will then be *in line* with the other two. If he is then asked to move and yet keep the two people always behind the other from where he is looking, he will notice that he can only move in a *straight line,* that is he cannot change his direction of movement except by going forward and then backward. This 'straight line' will *represent* the direction possessed by the line passing through the two positions at which the two people have placed themselves. These three people can then be allowed to move along, up and down, the straight line. If a fourth person comes along and looks at them all in line, and if he wishes to keep them all in line, he will have to join them walking up and down the straight line traced out by the first three, and so on.

To make the experience a little more general, we could use two pairs of people, the four positions taken up would lead eventually to the abstract idea of a quadrilateral. Let a fifth person walk around and stop as soon as one couple is so seen by him so that one member of the couple is behind the other. Then he should go on moving, keeping this couple in line with himself and try, at the same time, to get the other couple in line with himself. To do this he must get the members of this couple to be behind one another as seen from where he is. He will then have found a position which in the abstract can later be identified with the point of intersection of the two lines determined by the two pairs of points forming the 'vertices' (corners) of our quadrilateral.

There are many interesting games we can play with the idea of concurrence. Two lines are said to concur or meet at the point which they have in common. We could set up three couples, all three so placed that they are in line with a seventh person. We can naturally do this with more couples if we like. If we place ourselves at the point of concurrence and look at every single couple, each one will be seen in line with ourselves.

Let us take three such couples. Let us call them Ann and Adam, Beatrice and Bill, and Carol and Charles, so that Ann is behind Adam as seen from the point of concurrence, Beatrice is behind Bill as seen from the point of concurrence, and Carol is behind Charles as seen from the point of concurrence. Let us remember that we have now used seven people. Now let the six members of the three couples stay put and let another person find the intersection of the line Adam-Bill with the line Ann Beatrice. This could be the person X. Now the Person Y could stand at the intersection of the lines Beatrice-Carol and Bill-Charles. Finally person Z could stand where the lines Adam-Charles and Ann-Carol intersect. If we carry out this exercise fairly accurately, we will find that the persons designated by X, Y and Z are standing *in line with each other*.

We can repeat this exercise by introducing the idea of parallels. This can be done through the use of sunlight. If everybody follows his own shadow at any given point in time, they will be tracing out lines parallel to each other. So let us say that Ann is standing on Adam's shadow, or somewhere where Adam's shadow would be if he were much taller. Let us do the same for Bill and Beatrice, Beatrice will be standing on Bill's shadow, and equally Carol can be standing on Charles' shadow. If we then do the same exercise as before, in spite of the fact that we now have no point of concurrence for the lines Adam-Ann and Bill-Beatrice and Charles-Carol, we will still have the corresponding persons X, Y and Z in line.

Figure 65

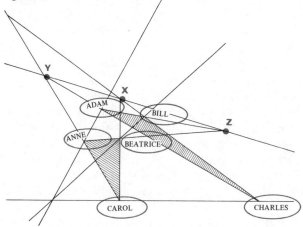

Shadow games

Some further interesting visual fun could be had by studying shadows. What kind of shadows can be cast by what kind of objects? It is fairly well known what kind of shadows a person can cast. If you are standing in a profile position with respect to the rays of the sun, you will have a shadow of your nose and your eyebrows and your mouth, but of course, you will never see this shadow, because as soon as you turn around to look at it, the shadow of your mouth disappears because you have the back of your head facing the sun. So you need to get someone else standing in profile, then you can look at his or her profile shadow.

Children find it fun to play shadow games on sheets. All sorts of interesting shapes can be made and quite terrifying or comical stories can be enacted for which some pretence movements can be carried out on the other side of the sheet, which are far less terrifying than they appear.

What kind of mathematics can be learnt from shadows? The reader might find it amusing to investigate what kind of shadows a cube can cast. It will be obvious that a cube can cast a square or rectangular shadow, but it seems stranger that it can also cast a *hexagonal* shadow. If we pick a cube up and hold it with two fingers along the opposite ends of a principal diagonal and shut one eye so that the diagonal is in line with the eye left open we will see a regular hexagon as the outline. This can be made even more convincing by arranging that the rays of the sun come parallel to one of these diagonals and that the shadow fall on a plane which is perpendicular to the rays of the sun. Since the sun is not overhead during any part of the day in most countries except in tropical ones, and since we cannot move the sun, we can nevertheless move the plane on which the shadow is cast. So take a piece of board and tilt it so that the rays of the sun hit the board perpendicularly, then a regular hexagonal shadow will be cast by the cube.

It is even easier to find out the kinds of shadows that a square can cast. Such a shadow could be a rectangle, a 'diamond' that is, a regular rhombus figure or a more general parallelogram. It is not generally known that with an equilateral triangle we can cast the shadow of a right angle triangle and vice versa. Any parallelogram, held at the required angle, will cast a square or a rectangular shadow. What we *cannot* do is to make a triangular shadow out of a square or conversely. A circular object can, of course, cast a circular shadow, but it can also cast an elliptical shadow.

It is fun to draw shadows on pieces of cardboard, and cut them out. We can then use the cut-out pieces of cardboard as further objects whose shadows we can then again draw on other pieces of cardboard and cut them out. So we can amuse ourselves by finding shadows of shadows, or shadows of shadows of shadows, and so on. For instance, it is an interesting problem whether the shadow of a shadow can be exactly the same shape as the one we started with, as well as exactly the same size? Can a shadow be the same shape as the one we start with, but smaller or larger? Is this possible? Or do we have to have the shadow of a shadow to achieve this feat?

To have more fun with shadows we can take a point source of light. For this we need a flashlight from which the reflector is taken off, so that the bulb only is used. This will be nearly a point source. We need, in addition, a darkened room. We will find that the square will now be able to cast not only parallelogram shadows but any other kind of quadrilaterals, and that the circle can cast not only circular and elliptical shadows, but also hyperbolic and parabolic shadows. As a matter of interest, it might be fun to study where they hyperbola turns into an ellipse. The ellipse on one side of the wall becomes bigger and bigger and bigger as we turn our circle round and will lose one part of it and become a hyperbola. This will happen just after it has passed through the *parabola stage*. The hyperbola stage continues as we turn our circular disc until the outline becomes very, very flat.

It is interesting to inquire what kinds of things still remain *unaltered* when you use flashlight as opposed to the kinds of things that remain unaltered when you use sunlight. For example, in the sunlight, parallels will remain parallel, but in the flashlight they will not. Nevertheless, there are certain things which do remain unaltered. The reader is referred to *Geometry Through Transformations, Volume I* (Dienes and Golding) for a more detailed account of these shadow phenomena.

Playing with symmetries

Making patterns

It's great fun to play with objects which have a certain number of lines of symmetry in them and seeing what kinds of constructions it is possible to make with them.

For example, let us take equilateral triangles. These can be cut out of all sorts of coloured cardboard. The problem can be posed as to what kinds of triangular or other shapes can be built out of them: big ones, little ones, middle ones, symmetrical ones, unsymmetrical ones, and so on.

Children have lots of fun using such sets of equilateral triangles for making pictures of human beings, dogs, flowers, and so on. They will also discover that they can make some beautiful stars. It is possible to make a star by using twelve equilateral triangles. You put six of them together to make what is known in geometry as a regular hexagon, and then at each side you put another triangle, and those will be the 'rays of light' emanating from the star. There will be six parts of the core of the star, and there will be six rays.

It is possible, of course, to make less symmetrical objects such as for example, triangles. Not many people would perhaps realize that it takes four triangles and not three to make another bigger triangle and then the next number is not eight but nine, unexpectedly. When it is being discovered that the next number after that is 16 an adult will jump to the idea that is must be 25 and 36 and 49 after that; the 'square numbers' turn out to be also 'triangle numbers'.

More children will argue quite differently, unless they have been spoilt by 'education', and will say something like this: 'Yes, here is one small triangle, I need three more to make a bigger triangle, that is $1 + 3 = 4$; then I need 5 more to make a bigger triangle, $4 + 5 = 9$; then I need 7 more to make a still bigger triangle, because $9 + 7 = 16$. So each time I need an odd number more, and it's always the next odd number more that I need, I need to add two more than I added before to get the next shape.'

In this way children learn that if they add successive odd numbers, they are going to get square numbers like $1 + 3 + 5 + 7 + 9 + 11 + 13 = 49$. It makes no difference where we stop, we always find a square number. By a 'square number' is meant the following, for those not initiated into the 'mysteries'. If you take such a number of pebbles, it is possible to set these pebbles out in the form of a square, that is to have as many rows in the pattern as there are pebbles in each row. This will result in a square looking shape.

It is also interesting to find the many other shapes that can be made out of triangles. For instance, it is possible to make a trapezium with the same proportions? The trapezium that can be made out of three equilateral triangles will have one side twice as long as the other sides. If these proportions are to be kept, then the next number of triangles to make a trapezium after 3 will be 12; after 12 it will be 36 and so on. In this way, we are constructing a mathematical function which is noted mathematically as 3 times x^2, where x is a number of units of length along the shorter side of the trapezium.

It is also fun to start with the trapezia and make triangles. It is easier of course to start with the triangles and make trapezia. So let us cut out a hundred or so trapezia. The base will be two inches long and the other three sides one inch long each. It will be quite difficult to find out in the beginning, how to make an equilateral triangle out of three of these trapezia.

Next problem: how to make another trapezoid out of four of these trapezia? It will be discovered that it takes again 9 or 16 or 25 or any square number of trapezia, to make a bigger trapezium.

If we put two equilateral triangles together we will make what is known as a *rhombus* in mathematics. We can cut out some rhombuses so that each side is one inch long, or two inches long. A square, of course, is a particular case of rhombus, where the angle between the sides is always the right angle. It will be found that again it takes a 'square number' of rhombuses to make another bigger rhombus. Then again, the sums of the first odd numbers will come in as an aid for the children.

In order to make the game more interesting, we might start by cutting bits out of our triangles and rhombuses. Let is take an equilateral triangle, and cut another smaller equilateral triangle out of it, so that the cut-out triangle reaches always the same point in the middle of the big triangle, in other words, let us always make the same shape.

What can we make out of these triangles? One shape will look like two legs; many ideas will suggest themselves such as: two legs, two arms and so on. We can make dogs, cats, people, out of these very simply constructed geometrical objects. Some more complex and so more interesting figures can also be made out of them. For example, here are some figures made, sometimes spontaneously, sometimes with a little guidance, by children of almost any age.

Figure 66

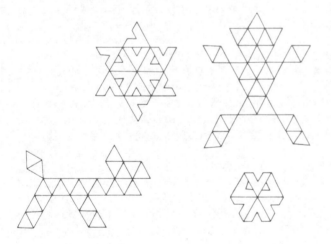

You will see that some of the pictures are symmetrical, in the sense that they are reflecting one side of the picture onto the other side. Some of the other pictures do not reflect. One has a kind of rotational aspect. It looks as though it is turning around. If we cut that figure out, put it on the table and then turned it around sixty degrees while you were not looking, you wouldn't know it has been turned, because the shape would be in apparently exactly the same position, even though it had been turned.

In the same way, some of the reflectional figures could be turned over their reverse sides without anybody noticing unless they had been looking. These properties of figures of being able to be moved without it being noticed that they have been move, are called *symmetries.* We see some rotational and some reflectional symmetries on the diagrams given.

The reader will readily see how to make some rotational and some reflectional symmetries out of triangles, out of squares, out of L shapes, out of parallelograms and so on. More interesting figures can be made out of parallelograms from which other parallelograms have been cut out or out of triangles from which triangles have been cut out and so on.

The sky is the limit for the kinds of things that it is possible to do with this kind of material.

Painting and cutting

But let us now go on to other types of symmetrical work. Let us take a pot of paint and some colours and take a square-shaped piece of paper. We can fold the square piece of paper along one of its diagonals, then along one of the other diagonals. The folds will now divide the square into four right-angled triangles. We can also fold along a line which joins the mid-points of the opposite sides. If we do both these further folds, we shall find that the square has been subdivided into eight small right-angled triangles.

We can now play the following game with the paints. Let us paint something in one of the eight spaces. Then let us say that before the paint dries, we are allowed to fold it over so that the paint prints over onto the other side of our piece of paper, and then fold it back again. We now have two pictures which are reflections of one another about the line which was the fold that we used for printing. Now, of course the paint will have dried, so we shall have to add another rule to the game namely that we are allowed to rewet or repaint anything that was printed before. In other words, we can put some more paint on what we have already painted but nowhere else and use another fold for printing the wet paint onto another part of the square. And again if anything gets dried up, we are allowed to repaint all the dry paint and refold again about another fold or about the same fold that we used before. In this way, eventually all the eight triangles will be painted over and we will see a beautiful symmetrical figure. Of course if we make an interesting figure in the first place it will be all the more interesting when it is printed in eight different regions of the square, looking highly organized as a structure.

We can do the same thing by giving the child a piece of paper cut out in the form of a regular hexagon or in the form of an equilateral triangle. In the case of the regular hexagon, there are six folds which we can use, namely the joins of the mid-points of the opposite sides as well as the joins of the opposite corners. All these will make satisfactory folds. This will give us 12 different right-angled triangles in which to paint. There will be lots of rewetting of the paint and folding. We shall end up with a very flower like structure when we have finished all the painting.

Figure 67

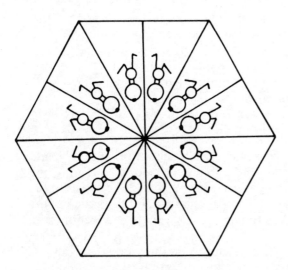

To do the same thing with a triangle, is a little more difficult, but not impossible. We have to fold along the line which joins a corner of the triangle to the mid-point of the opposite side. There are three of these folds. All these folds will meet, or course, in the middle of the triangle. Thus we shall have made six regions in the triangle in which we can paint. We can repeat the painting, folding, repainting, folding game until all the six triangles are printed on.

Instead of painting, it might be fun to do some cutting. Take a pair of scissors, and take a square which has been folded and folded and folded, about three consecutive folds: it looks like this

Figure 68

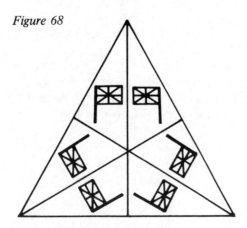

Now get a pair of scissors, very pointed, and very sharp, and cut right through the eight layers of paper to make one figure. This could be any figure you choose, such as a person, or a dog, or a flower, or any kind of abstract shape you wish. When you have unfolded the paper you will see miraculously that you have created a similar effect to the one created by the printing.

Again similar effects can be created by folding the hexagon or folding the equilateral triangle will give very surprising kinds of effects.

There are other ways in which we can play with symmetries. We need not stay in a *plane* but expand in space itself. We usually play with symmetry every morning when we shave. In the mirror we see the reflection of ourselves and so the plane of the mirror generates a transformation of the world in which we live, into its reverse, to form a world which Lewis Carroll has described in his famous book 'Alice Through the Looking Glass'.

Many interesting games can be played through the looking glass. For example, traffic would proceed on the opposite side of the road, clocks will go round the wrong' way, and all sorts of things like that will be happening in looking glass land. Not to mention the problem of what happens when you look in the mirror in Looking Glass Land itself!

Use of everyday objects: reflections

Even without having a natural looking glass we can pretend to have one. Take a number of pieces of furniture. You would probably need about eight pieces which have the same shape, such as chairs. Take eight kitchen chairs which are of the same shape and size and establish a 'road' in the middle of the room. Say to your child that you want a house built on one side of the road. Tell him not to use more than four of the eight chairs. He can put the chairs upside down, sideways, back to front, at an angle, just any way he likes as long as he doesn't block up the roadway, so that his cars can go back and forth in the road. Then you say, having duly praised his efforts: 'It would be rather nice to have a house on the opposite side of the road exactly the same as the one you have just built on this side, so that when you walk down the road what you see on the left hand side of the road, you should see in exactly the same way on the right hand side of the road'.

This is surprisingly difficult for quite a lot of people to do. Two chairs being placed looking exactly the same, on the left and on the right will be interpreted as having pushed one chair over onto the other side of the road. This will not do, of course, because the chair will have to

Figure 69

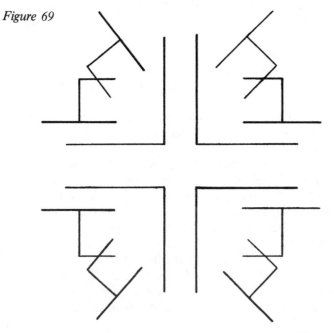

be turned over as well, to make it look the same as it did before when looked at from the centre of the road! We are really creating a *reflection image* of the first house, using the road, as a camouflage, for a mirror.

Later, we might suggest that it is not very interesting to have just two houses in the town, we ought to have at least four. We may imagine a crossroads: one road going, say, north to south, and the other road going east to west. If we put one of our houses in one corner of the crossroads, then we suggest that we use only two chairs for this now, unless there are lots and lots of chairs available. The house that is built will have to be copied on the other side of the north-south road as well as on the other side of the east-west road. Having copied them both, there is still a fourth house to build which has to be on the other side of the east-west and of the north-south road, that is diagonally across the crossroads with the first house we built. Miraculously enough, this fourth house can be built so that it reflects the second as well as the third house about the two roads respectively. In other words, we shall finish up with the eight chairs making up four houses using two chairs for each house.

Then, it's quite fun to get into the house. If there are four of you, like mother, father, and two children or just four children, one of you can get into the house, and sit on one of the chairs in some way. Then, you can say: 'I want another person on the other side of the street doing exactly the same thing as I am doing', and so, this other person will have to do the reflection image of what you are doing on the other side of the north-south street: but you need yet another person to do what you are doing on the other side of the east-west street, as well. Then this second and third person will need a fourth person to copy what they are doing again on the other side of the north-south and the east-west streets. These four players can take it in turns to move themselves around into different positions and the remaining three have to reflect the new positions across the street from which they are looking at the original person. There will of course, be always one person that isn't a reflection of the first person. He is the one who is sitting or standing diagonally opposite the first person across the crossroads. He will be the reflection of a reflection.

It won't be long before it is discovered that the first house, and the one which is diagonally opposite the intersection can be transformed into one another *not by reflection* but by *turning it half way around.* Standing in the middle of the intersection, I could pick up the first house, turn myself half way round and put it down on the opposite corner, and it will occupy exactly the same space, and will look exactly the same as that opposite house was when I built it. In other words, the reflection of the reflection can be carried out as a turn (or rotation, as we say in mathematics).

There is, of course, no need to bother about these mathematical details as we play the games. These insights will come soon enough as we begin to realize how to make constructions more and more effectively.

It will eventually occur to one of the children that they might have more than two streets in the village. Now, it depends whether we want three streets or four streets as to what we have to do next. If we wish to have three streets all meeting in one main intersection in the middle of the village, then these streets will divide the village into six sections and the streets will make angles of 60 degrees with one another. If we wish to have four streets, then the angle between the streets will be 45 degrees, that is one half of a right angle. The 45 degrees one is the easiest to start with. It is suggested that if the 60 degree game is played, the streets be represented by masking tape being placed along the floor in the middle of each of the three streets, making sure that the angle between the streets is as nearly as possible 60 degrees, that is, one sixth of a whole turn. If we then place a house in one of the six sections, then we have to reflect across the street on one side of the house, and across the other street on the other side of the house. Then, we go on reflecting until we are back at the first house. In the end, we will find that we have no embarassment when we meet the original house again. It will finally reflect back into itself if we have not made any mistakes in the construction. The same remarks apply to constructions where the streets are at an angle of 45 degrees, that is, one half of the right angle with one another.

Figure 70

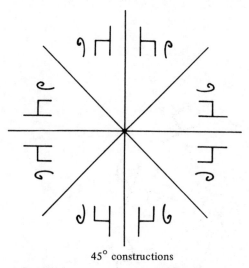

45° constructions

It will be seen that to construct situations in which reflectional symmetries are realized, involve a *left to right identification*. Assuming you are on one of the 'streets', what is on your left must be seen and felt exactly in the same way on your right.

Figure 71

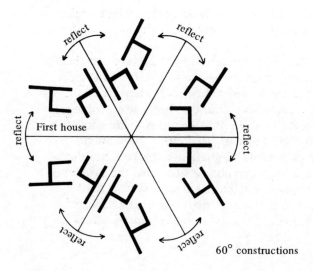

60° constructions

Rotational constructions

There is no need to play the game in just this way. We may for example decide to have a circular space in the middle of the village. Let someone stand in the middle of this circle, and look at a house on the edge of this circle; suppose he makes a certain turn about himself, say a quarter of a full turn, but still stays in the middle of the circle, and suppose that he wishes to see exactly the same sort of house in front of him as he did before he turned! In other words, the left-hand side of the first house he looked at will have to look just like the left-hand side of the second house he is looking at now after he has made his turn; the right-hand side of the first house will have to look just like the right-hand side of the second house. This was not so just now because the left-hand had to look like the right, and right had to look like the left, as can be seen on the diagrams provided.

Figure 72   *Figure 73*

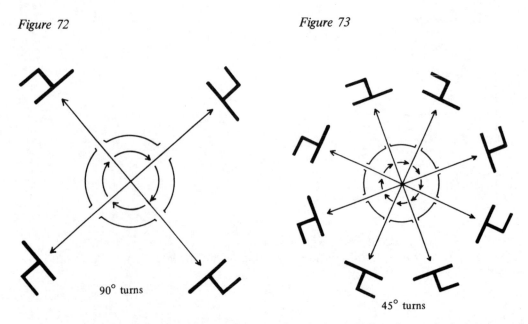

If the angle through which we turn ourselves in the middle of our circle is, say a right-angle, or 45 degrees, we shall get the kind of picture shown on Figures 72 and 73. If the angle is 45 or 60 degrees, we shall get the type of pictures shown in Figure 74.

It will be seen that if we walk along the streets indicated by the lines in the picture, we shall not see the same thing on the right as on the left, because we have made a left to left, and right to right identification, whereas before we made a left to right, and right to left identification. This causes a considerable amount of muddle, which is interesting muddle, because a problem is always interesting. Part of the interest is to unmuddle the muddle. In order to provide some fun, we always have to create a certain amount of difficulty. Without any difficulty there are no problems, and without any problems, there is no fun. If there is no challenge, there is no game. So clearly the games that we play, have to be tailored to our own abilities to solve the problems which we put into the games. The problem of transferring our attention from a left to right identification, to left left, and right right identification, is a piece of mental gymnastics which makes our thinking more supple in the same way as physical gymnastics makes our physical muscles more supple.

Figure 74

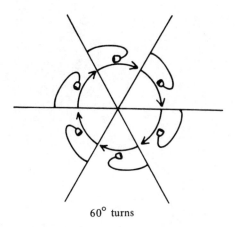

60° turns

  The problem now arises as to whether we can have our cake and eat it. We know that it is possible to construct a figure in which we do see the same thing on the right and on the left, as we go down the street. It is also possible to construct a figure with a 'middle', such that if we stand in the middle and look at a house, then turn around and look at the next house, but without moving away from the middle, we do see a house looking just like the first house. But can we construct a figure in which we can do both of these things? In other words, can we have left to left, right to right identification at the same time as left to right, right to left identification? Strangely enough, this is possible, but of course, it restricts even more the ways in which you can put the chairs down. It will be noticed that a normal chair has a plane of symmetry right across its middle. If we sit in a chair, our right leg and our left leg have similar supports to rest on. Our right hand and our left hand will be able to feel exactly the same things up and down the chairs; so the chair itself is symmetrical about a vertical plane passing through its middle. If this plane of symmetry also goes through the middle of our figure, then we will find that we will have eaten our cake and still have it, because we can turn while staying in the middle of the figure, and still see a chair in front of us that looks just like the chair we saw before we turned. We can also walk down the streets between the chairs and look to our left, and look to our right, and we will still see the same thing on both sides of us. Of course, we will have smuggled in some more roads, if by roads we mean planes of symmetry. We will have made twice as many such 'roads' as we had to start with. If we started off with two roads, that means we have put our chairs in the four corners facing each other or else back to back to each other, but in any case in such a way that the planes of symmetry of the chairs themselves pass through the middle of the construction. Exactly the same thing will happen if we started with six chairs (that is with three roads). We will have introduced three more roads but these roads go bang on through the houses. You have to go through the front door, and out the back door if you want to follow that kind of road. We can try by climbing up the chairs, and jumping over the back of them. As we do so, we will still see the same thing on our right as on our left, including the bits of the chairs on which we are climbing, as well as all the other chairs which we have placed (Figure 77).

Figure 75

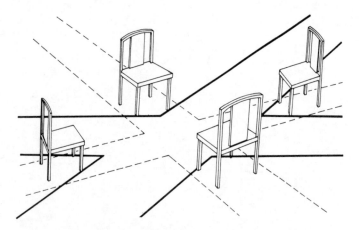

Getting away from regularity

So far, we have played with very regular types of shapes. We have been thinking about squares, triangles, and so on. We have handled straight roads, planes, representing mirrors reflecting exactly one side of the world into its opposite side inside the looking glass, and so on. Of course, in mathematics and in other human forms of expression, we do not stop at such idealized ways of expressing ourselves.

As a first stage of departing from the very regular, take a square and cut a circle out of it. Out of this circle cut out a square. Out of this square we can cut out a circle, and out of this circle a square. We can in this way construct a sequence where the pieces will be getting smaller and smaller since each piece is cut out of the previous one. Naturally, we don't need to leave the pieces in the same order. We can let our imagination run away with us, and make all sorts of interesting shapes with the circle and the square motifs. In exactly the same way, we can cut out triangles out of squares, and then squares out of triangles. or we can use three different shapes. We could start with a square, out of that cut a circle; out of the circle a triangle, out of the triangle a square, and so on, until the shapes get so small that we would find it difficult to cut any more out. Naturally, it's good to start with a very large piece of paper or piece of cardboard so that we have a large number of piece to play with in the end. (Figures 76 and 77).

Figure 76

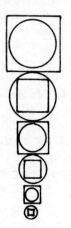

Figure 77

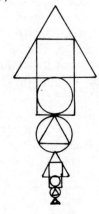

It is also good to have several different colours. We might start with three or four different coloured squares and cut them up in different ways and then, the numbers of ways in which we can combine these to make shapes is practically unlimited. In this way, by combining conventional shapes in quite unconventional ways, we can already get out of the restrictions into which the very simple type of mathematics has been keeping us enclosed.

It would be better still to break out of the regular geometrical forms as well. We can make up all sorts of different shapes out of curves. For example, take four or five sheets of transparent paper or plastic and draw different shapes on these. Then put them on top of one another, and see what kinds of effects you can create. Naturally, some of the curves would go well with some of the other curves, like some of them would go inside, some of them touch one another, some of them would intersect, depending on how we placed our pieces of transparent paper or plastic together.

If we decided that every drawing would have to have just one inside and one outside, that is, it would be just one closed curve, it would place a certain restriction on the way in which we could draw our figures. But we would still have quite a lot of freedom; it is surprising how many different closed curves it is possible to make, and how little we are really restricted by such a restriction. Here are some examples of what is possible and the reader is invited to invent others and superimpose them on one another to make the most interesting kinds of shapes.

Figure 78   *Figure 79*

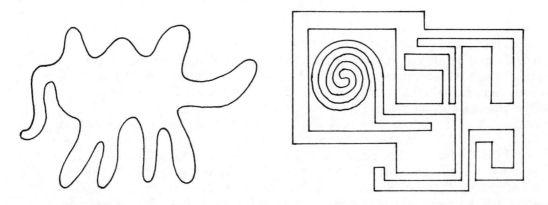

Many different maze games can be constructed out of such shapes. Naturally, it is not necessary to restrict ourselves to having just an inside and an outside. Here is a maze, Fig. 80, in which there are three different regions so that if you happen to be in one region, you can only catch people that are in the same region unless, of course, you have a key to a door. Now, there are two doors in the maze, and you would have to find which door you would have to have the key to for catching another 'person'.
'Persons' can be placed at any place 'inside' or 'outside' the maze. Where is the inside of it?

What do you have to do in order to get from one person to another? It would be possible for instance, to throw a dice for the keys, and see whether using that door a player can go from one person to the other. If he can, he wins the point, if he cannot he loses, and so it's the next players' turn to throw the dice, and see if he or his representative point can move along the maze to another chosen person. The chosen person can also be determined by throwing another dice on which the names of the 'persons' are written. In other words, we could have six doors and six persons, or we could have three doors and the keys to the doors would be symbolized by letters or colours or shapes, as the case may be, and written on the faces of a small cube used as a die.

Figure 80

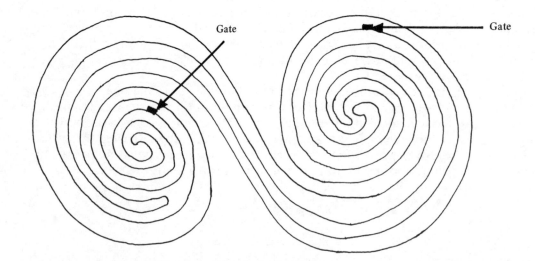

Gate

Gate

The fun about these games is that we ourselves construct the situation, and then explore the possibilities of getting from place to place. The person who has drawn the maze very often forgets how to get from place to place, and he himself is often not in a better position than the other players who didn't know how the maze was originally constructed.

Another way of playing with the mazes would be to say that you could only walk along the walls, that is along the 'lines'. Two mazes can be put on top of one another, each one having been drawn on a piece of transparent paper or plastic, and then, the intersections of the lines would be marked. People would be facing each other along the walls, and each person would have to stand at one of the intersections. The number of intersections you are allowed to pass could be determined by the throw of the dice, or in any other way we might think fit. This would be equivalent to playing catch out of doors, when it might be a rainy afternoon or you might be stuck in a snowstorm.

In this game it will be found that if somebody is walking around an entirely different wall from somebody else, he can never be caught unless, of course, he is allowed to 'change walls' at the intersections. We can vary the rules by saying you are allowed to change walls only once, or that you are not allowed to change walls at all; or let's say we are only allowed to change walls if we throw a double on one of the dice when we throw for the number of intersections we can pass.

Children, parents and teachers will have fun constructing different variants of these games. The construction and the superposition of the different mazes will give an outlet for creative expression on the part of the child, as clearly the actual shape of the maze is irrelevant. What counts is just whether you can get in or out of the maze. Individual expression for making this kind or that kind of a maze can be allowed absolutely free rein, and yet the mathematical content of the game would still remain the same.

6. How do we learn?

Possible roles of the sense-modalities

In the last few chapters we have suggested a number of exercises and games that can be played by children or adults, in the home or at school. Some of these had the appeal of moving the body around in the form of dancing or gymnastics. Others used the sense of touch, and still others sight, that is, the awareness of colour and form. So now the reader might be beginning to wonder how all these types of exercises contribute to the emerging picture. How do we really learn things that are abstract, that are difficult, that are complex?

Every one of us, at one stage or another in his life, has to learn quite a number of difficult, complex, and abstract notions. Take, for example, a garage mechanic. He does not just have to learn how to service a certain given model of car, or how to repair certain damage that might have happened to a certain particular car, but to cars in general, because anybody might come in with any kind of a car, even a foreign car that he has never seen. What does he do? If he has some grey matter, and is willing to use it, he will say to himself, 'Oh, yes. Cars on the whole work in this way. There must be a water-pump somewhere. There must be a carburettor,' and so on. And so he looks for the usual kind of circuits, the usual components, that every car must have. He will realize that the particular ways these are put together are matters of detail. The principle of how the internal combustion engine can be combined with locomotion is something which a good garage mechanic must know. This is *abstract knowledge*. Since it is abstract, it is applicable over a very wide field. Abstract means in this connection that the principle in question is not tied to very specific, very concrete or special kinds of exemplars of the principle. In other words, in an abstract principle we have rid ourselves of particularities, of the concreteness, and we are able to achieve a certain amount of detachment. Consequently, the abstract principle or knowledge can be seen to apply to just those bits and pieces of concrete experience which are judged appropriate. This universality is the power of abstraction.

Mathematics, par excellence, is more abstract than any other discipline. Consequently it is more applicable than any other discipline. It is a truism to say that mathematical models are being used increasingly in almost every walk of the industrial, scientific, political, and economic life of the world. People are beginning to realize the power of mathematical analysis, in other words the power of the abstract over the concrete.

In this chapter, we would like to suggest that we can take our knowledge of learning a little further, since we have now been through a certain number of learning experiences. If the reader has carried out even some, if not all, of the exercises contained in the previous chapters, he will enjoy the heady satisfaction of distilling their essence from the chapters that follow. Learning takes place through coming into contact with situations. If varied situations are not occuring with any degree of frequency, we have no problems and we do not learn anything. It is when things change that we need to learn. Learning means adapting to new situations.

An animal learns when he is put in a new environment. He learns how to get on in it, find his food in it, fight for his territorial rights in it. If we wish to learn, or wish somebody else to learn, one way of making sure that this will happen is to arrange the environment in such a way that the learner will meet many varied situations.

We have taken the sense modalities in a certain order. This particular order is of interest in describing how we learn or how we might best learn. Probably the first connection we have with the world is moving ourselves around in it, or at least moving our arms and legs around in it. We have to establish a connection between our body and the rest of the world. This connection needs to be perfected, if indeed we wish to survive. The coordination of bodily movement with the displacement of the body in space are of paramount importance for adapting ourselves to the world, which comes to the same thing as learning about the world. Learning means adapting to many varied and changing circumstances. This is what we tried to show in the first and the second chapters, where we showed how bodily movement can be used to serve the process of learning. Even in the third chapter, where rhythmical considerations were introduced, we were still at the stage of using the body as the principal agent for learning.

The sense of touch was taken as the next possible sense modality which should be called into play. Much later came the sense of sight. We suggest that there may be something to be said for observing a certain order, or at least a certain order of importance, in selecting different sense modalities as principal learning agents. It goes without saying that in the schoolrooms very little is learned through the movement of the body. Most schoolrooms are compulsorily quiet. The children are sitting, being very good, in rows of desks. They do not move, do not touch, and perhaps do not even see. Possibly they *only hear* and certainly in addition, they *fear*. Small wonder that the necessary adaptation takes place painfully slowly. It is a testimony to the resilience of the human spirit that some people get through the horrors of scholastic experience sufficiently undamaged to be able to contribute effectively to future adaptations in adult life.

The first four stages of learning

We might consider the initial attempts at adaptation to the environment, as a *first stage of learning*. When the organism is young, this takes the form of *play*. All young creatures play. They need to do this in order to acquire the skills which are necessary for survival in adult life. Muscular co-ordination has to be learned as this leads to walking, to reaching, and to getting things or throwing them away, or eating things or spitting things out. All these are skills which need to be learned to perfection to adapt to a changing set of circumstances in a constantly changing environment.

The first stage of learning, then, is play. This is a spontaneous adaptation to the environment in which we find ourselves. The child plays with his own body. He also plays with objects around him. When he plays with his own body, he explores what he has to wield. He also explores various sensations that he can cause to himself by rocking the chair, by swinging the swing, by swimming, by running, by riding the bicycle. All these are sensations which he enjoys and which he can produce by movement of certain muscles in the body. All these are preparatory play, which enable him to use his muscles. Or, as he grows, he may engage in more complex muscular activities, such as dancing, hockey, tennis or anything else of the kind.

As we adapt to the environment by moving, by touching, by seeing, eventually we discover that there are certain regularities. Certain things always seem to happen in certain ways but not in other ways. Certain things are possible to do and others are not. These regularities lead us to the idea that somehow the world is structured according to rules. Whether this is indeed so or not, we shall never know. But it surely appears so. It is not long before we start making up our own rules. This means that we have invented our first *game*. A game is determined by the restrictions that we impose on ourselves and a goal we set that we must reach while the restrictions remain in force. In a game of chess we cannot move our pieces just anywhere, and it is because of such restrictions that it remains a game. In tennis you cannot just throw the ball anywhere, you have to hit it in a certain place, and in a certain way, and it must not touch the net, and it must not do this, that or the other. When certain things have happened a certain number of times according to the rules, the game is over, and another can be started. It is the use of the regularities imposed upon ourselves that makes the activities interesting and intricate. In the exercises explained in the previous chapters, it is the restrictions imposed that generate the fun. Manipulation under rule-bound conditions could be considered as the *second stage* of learning.

It is not necessary that a game should have a goal in the way of winning.

Some games are exploratory, where we merely explore what gives. After such exploration, we can make up a winning-losing game, which satisfies another side of us, namely the love of meeting a challenge. Such challenges develop *strategies* in our minds and the best strategist becomes the expert player. We will not make any moral judgement about what kind of games are the best games to play. Some people like to play more freely, others simply like to follow a certain set of rules and play against another person, and play to win. In general we might regard the invention of rules, or of playing along by the rules, as a *second stage* in learning. This could include a certain amount of freedom in changing the rules, or in inventing other games altogether. Most of the games that are described in the previous chapters come under this category, except in a few cases where we have gone a little bit further. In some cases, it will be remembered, games of the same structure have been compared to each other. We have played some rhythmical games, and we have suggested that alongside certain rhythmical changes, we could play a dance game or another tactile game. So, in other words, the moves in one game could trigger off corresponding moves in another very similar game in which the inner 'hanging-togetherness' of the moves is just the same in one as in the other game. If this were not so, we could not choose moves in one game to trigger off the corresponding moves in the other.

When such a detailed comparison or identification of one game with another takes place, we are reaching to a higher level or learning. We are beginning to look underneath the game and see what it is made of. Instead of driving the car, we become curious and look under the hood. Irrespective of the particular move that we have to make, we are looking at the relationships between the moves. In order to see this relationship clearly, we have to get rid of the concrete properties of the moves themselves, because these properties will get in the way of our considerations of the relations *between* the moves. So in order to learn more about the abstract nature of the relationships between moves, we have suggested that we play a number of different games and that we compare them. For instance, the 'last shall be first' move in the permutation game is likened to the 'going on' move in one of the rhythm games. The 'reversal' in the rhythm games, again, is likened to one of the 'exchanging' moves in the permutation game.

As soon as we do this kind of thing we are pitting one whole set of relations against another set of relations and we try to find out if the first set of relations is, in fact, really quite identical to the second. We try to 'map' one game onto another, and map that game onto the first game, so that for each thing we do in one there is a corresponding thing we do in the other, and it all fits like hand fits glove, then we can begin to forget about the bits and pieces which make the game into that particular one. This comparing activity could be called the third stage of learning. During this stage we begin to deal with the abstract nature of the relations. We begin, in fact, to learn some *mathematics*, and cease to play with the concrete. We begin to *play with* our own construction. This construction is the set of relationships which makes each game what it is.

After we extract something which is common to a number of different activities, and having decided that all these activities are really the same kind of thing, we are in a difficult position. We seem to have learned something which is common to all of these various activities we know, but we do not know what this thing is that they do have in common. In other words, we have learned something which is nameless, which is shapeless, which does not have any kind of a peg on which to hang it. We have somehow internalized something which we feel is the same in a number of different activities, but now having internalized it, we do not know how to look at it, we do not know how to talk about it.

In order to use this knowledge, we ought to be able to take it out of ourselves and put it down on paper, or in some way image it, picture it, represent it. So, having gone through the third stage of learning, the finding of the common things between the concrete things which are alike in our activities, we are now crying out for a fourth stage which will allow us somehow to make a picture of what we have learned. And it is this fourth stage which is quite crucial in learning mathematics, and, as with the third stage, is usually left out of most mathematics textbooks and most mathematics learning situations.

It is the conviction of the author that, if more attention were paid to the way in which abstract ideas were learned, or could be learned by most people, then abstractions in mathematics could become the plaything of the majority of people, rather than remain the preserve of a small but powerful mathematical aristocracy.

In the rest of this chapter we will not try to give the full answer to the question posed in the title of the chapter, namely how we learn, but we shall just try to take the matter one stage further. We will try to pull out of the games described some common properties, then suggest ways in which these common properties can be pictured, in representational forms. Such a representation could be used for any one of the appropriate games without actually saying which one. When using a representation, we only talk about the relationships in the games and not about the actual games themselves. And we shall then be able to go into a study of these relationships in detail, and use a suitable *language* which will be the language of mathematics.

It is this language which has, so far, remained foreign to most people, simply because the study of the learning of mathematics, up to quite recent years, was not ever undertaken in any scientific manner, nor has it been possible to obtain any considerable amount of foundation or government funds for the study of such learning, because such learning has never been considered a phenomenon which is capable of any kind of scientific investigation. Hopefully, the days of such rank prejudices are passing, and very soon governments, industry, and private foundations will see their way to granting more and more funds to competent teams of researchers, who, will then be able to find ways by means of which the learning of mathematics can be made available to the vast majority of the people in the world.

Representations in counting and adding

We shall now pinpoint in some detail how we can pass from the stage of comparison to the stage of representation and thus rid ourselves of considerable amounts of flotsam which might still be getting in the way of our own abstracting.

Let us consider the problem of drawing houses with differently coloured windows. We could have a succession of houses such as those in fig.81, and we can recall a 'similar' series of tactile sensations where the dots show where the fingers are touched, (fig.82).

Figure 81

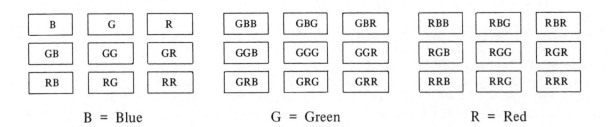

B	G	R		GBB	GBG	GBR		RBB	RBG	RBR
GB	GG	GR		GGB	GGG	GGR		RGB	RGG	RGR
RB	RG	RR		GRB	GRG	GRR		RRB	RRG	RRR

B = Blue   G = Green   R = Red

Figure 82

It will not take long to see that the two series are very similar; one is made out of colours, the other out of feelings of touch. A game could be played by touching somebody's fingers in a certain way and the person touched would have to draw the house with the 'right' number of windows and with the colours arranged in the 'right' way. But what does 'right' mean in this case? If we keep the *same order* as the one given on the diagrams, we obtain the following obvious correspondences:

No fingers touched : one blue window in house
Index finger only touched : one non-blue window in house
Middle finger touched but
ring finger not touched : two windows in house
Ring finger touched : three windows
Tip of finger : green window
Base of finger : red window

Finger not touched (to the
left of any finger being
touched)   :   blue window
Index finger shows colour of window on furthest right
Middle finger shows colour of window second from the right
Ring finger shows colour of window third from the right.

We can represent both the above series by means of the 'trees' in **Fig.** 83.

It is easily seen now that both trees have the same 'structure', and that this is why it is possible to 'translate' one order into the order by means of the correspondences given earlier. It will also be not too difficult to see that we can fill out such a tree by the base three counting game in which we use *a thumb* to mean *one,* an *index finger* to mean *three,* and a middle finger to mean *nine.*

On the 'tree' in fig.84 we can see that we can 'count' from zero to 26 using again the very same structure as for the other two series. The picture of our tree can therefore be used to *represent* any ordering of 27 objects, real or abstract, which are thought of as split up into 'sub-orders' of nine and of three, inside the overall order in which we imagine our 27 objects.

Finally, we can use the tree, *stripped of its content,* as an *abstract representation* of any activity of the kind we have been considering. It will then become possible to study the abstraction, without having to bother with the tiresome detail of what it was that led us to the abstraction.

Figure 83

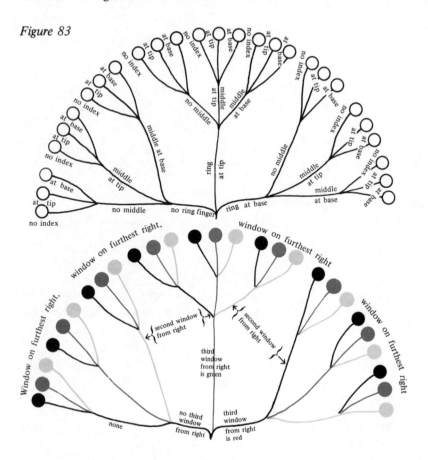

Figure 84

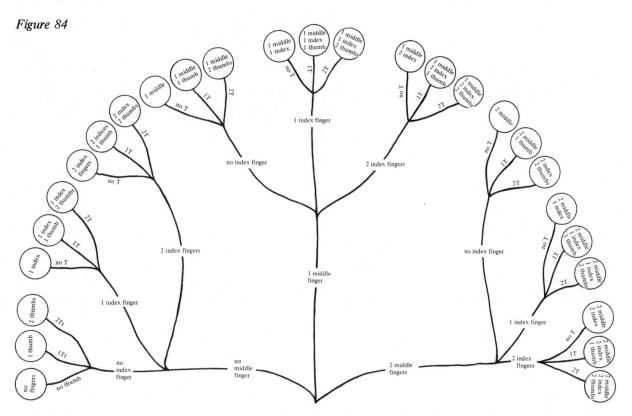

It is a very useful and necessary trick to find a *representation of an abstraction,* because abstractions do not really exist, and so we have to give them a temporary and spurious existence in order to study them.

Let us now find some schemata for the adding situations in base three in which we used thumbs, index fingers, middle fingers, and ring fingers. We can draw the end points of the branches of the tree along an indefinitely produced straight line. Since we do not need to draw any trees, only end points, we can continue, or at least imagine continuing, indefinitely from left to right the accumulated numbers of fingers. If, in the process, we reach the little finger, we can go on to the thumb of the other hand until we reach the little finger of that hand. Then we can go on to toes, and so on, at least in our imagination. On the first rules we can observe the regular succession of 'amounts' shown starting with zero, going on to one thumb, then to two thumbs, then one index finger, one index finger with thumb, and so on, until we reach right past the ring finger. In Fig. 85 we can see that between thin vertical lines there is always an index-finger's worth of difference, that is a difference of three. If we look at the division, just one beyond a vertical line, and if we want to go to where one index-finger's worth more is shown, we pass the next vertical line on the right and take one more. If we are two divisions to the right of a thin vertical line, to have an index-finger's worth more, we pass the next thin vertical line and·take two more divisions after that. Similarly, if we want to find the position with one middle-finger-more, we either go from one dark vertical line to the next dark vertical line or we pass a vertical and we go the same distance to the right of this as the distance we were to the right of the one next to which we started.

101

Figure 85

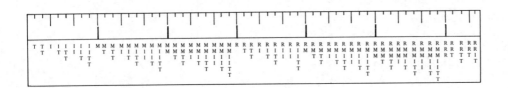

Figure 86

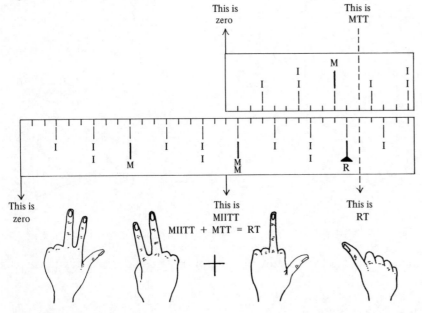

MIITT + MTT = RT

To sum up:

to 'add' one thumb's worth : move one division to the right

to 'add' one index finger's worth : pass a thin vertical line and stop at similar relative position to where you move from

to 'add' a middle finger's worth : pass a dark vertical line and stop at similar relative position to where you move from.

For instance, consider the following sum:

middle thumb thumb + middle index index thumb thumb.

We start at the point shown by middle thumb thumb and then pass one black vertical line, pass two thin vertical lines and then take two more divisions towards the right. Another simple way of doing these 'additions' would be to make two rulers, each of them being scaled accurately in units of equal length. Let us call them ruler A and ruler B. All we have to do is to mark the spot on ruler A where our first quantity to be added is represented, put the zero position of ruler B against this spot, run our finger up ruler B until we reach the amount represented by our second quantity on this ruler and then see at what division we have arrived on our first ruler. Just such a slide rule operation, as it might be called, is shown in Fig. 86 where middle thumb thumb is, so to speak, added to middle index index thumb thumb:

102

Three of the four thumbs are worth an index finger, which gives three index fingers. Three index fingers are worth a middle finger, and so we really have three middle fingers, which are worth a ring finger. This is how we get RING, THUMB. It is much quicker on the slide rule. The only problem is that one has to understand it to use it.

Naturally, there is no need to restrict ourselves to base three operations. We can make these rulers in base four or in base five, or even, of course, in the usual base ten. Here are some diagrams to illustrate such slide rules in these different bases, which can easily be made out of stiff cardboard with a thin ballpoint pen to help us mark the points.

Figure 87

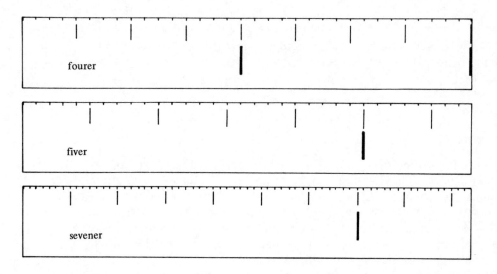

Children will amuse themselves for long periods of time in doing adding exercises with such slide rules.

Naturally, subtracting exercises can also be carried out, but then, of course, instead of *moving up* we shall have to *move down*. We shall have to put the zero position of slide rule B again against the quantity required on the ruler A from which we subtract. Ruler B will need to have its scale placed in the opposite sense from that of ruler A. In that case, we can do some easy subtracting exercises. Again, this can be done in bases three, four, five, or ten, or any others that might be fancied.

This little trick of representing numbers by the number of little dots that we have passed from a certain initial starting position called zero is a very useful trick. In modern mathematics books, such a representation is known as the *number line*. It is, however, somewhat dangerous, in the author's opinion, to use the number line too freely until one has understood just exactly what it does. The number of spaces we count, starting from the zero position, is the number which measures our quantity we wish to use in terms of distance.

Measure already makes use of number. If a child does not as yet understand fully how numbers work, it would be somewhat dangerous to try to get him to learn this through the use of measure. It is truly like getting the cart to pull the proverbial horse. How can he measure something in so many units, unless he knows what numbers really do? When we measure something we count the number of units of the type that we happen to have chosen, that fit along a certain line. The number gives a measure of this count. It is hard to imagine that the measure can be used to *learn* about counting since you have to know how to count and understand what the counting numbers 1, 2, 3, 4, ... are, before any measuring can be done. Once, however, numbers and their properties, and the processes of adding and subtracting, have been understood in principle, then such number lines and the accompanying 'measures' are an extremely useful way of representing this abstract idea of number. Properties of the abstraction obtained can then be deduced from the diagram, although great care should be taken that the representation is not confused with the abstraction which it represents. The dots that are t marked on the line are not the numbers. These dots merely represent numbers. Nor is the distance from the zero point a number. That is a distance only, which is *measured* by means of our number, if we choose as our unit the distance between two consecutive small, thin lines.

The above are words of warning for parents or teachers who might be tempted to use representations as initial learning situations by means of which to introduce mathematical abstractions such as numbers.

Representations in other games

Now let us go back to some of the other games that we have played, such as the three-cornered waltz, the other dances, the rhythmical games, and so on. We have seen that a number of these have certain things in common, and that it is possible to identify some of these games with others move by move, so that when something happens in one game an exactly corresponding thing would happen in the other. So that, apart from the content, the way in which the moves hang together in the two different games are really the same. This is what is meant by saying that the structure is the same in both cases.

There must be some way in which we can *represent* this kind of structure so that we can look at it from the outside, talk about it, express the kind of game it is, and possibly make up a sorting exercise. Such sorting would enable us to say just why certain games belonged to this category, and others to other categories. This is essentially what we do when we are very young and learn to distinguish between different shapes, different colours, different kinds of flowers, different kinds of people, and so on. We learn to *discriminate*. We learn that some objects or events are different from other objects or events, and yet some are rather similar to each other. In other words, we put things in categories. The objects or events that come in the same category are somehow judged similar for reasons often not too clear to us. These reasons may of course become clear later. To some readers the similarities between some of the games will already stand out. In the remaining part of this chapter, we shall suggest some procedures through which the sorting into kinds of game can be accomplished more readily.

Let us take the three-cornered waltz. There are six different positions in which the dancers can be. These are represented in Fig. 88, which can be considered to be a *map*.

Now let us say that we are in one of these spaces on the map. When we see that 'we are here' on a map, we clearly do not mean this literally. A space on the map will represent a position of the dancers. The passage from one space to another space will represent the move or the dance step, or steps, that allow the dancers to pass from one particular position to another particular position. If we take the left step, for example, as one of the movements we are going to represent, then this left step will join three of the positions together, assuming we start with

Figure 88

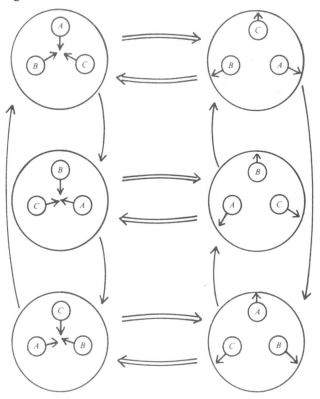

one particular position. So whatever position we start from, when we have done the left step three times, one after the other, we shall be back to our starting position. This is true of whatever position we start with. Although we find that there are three positions which can be reached from each other by doing left steps, the other three can never be reached unless we do a twiddle. So the six positions are divided into two sets of three which are essentially different from each other. We saw that three of these positions were characterized by the dancers facing inwards, and the other three by them facing outwards.

We can reach an inward facing position from an outward facing position, or the other way around, by doing a twiddle. We can choose one particular twiddle which will be represented by an arrow going from one row to the other row in the diagram. Let us take the boy's twiddle in the version of the game where we have one boy and two girls.

We have a neat diagram which represents this particular game. Can this diagram be made to represent another game which is similar in structure, but different in content? Let us go back to a rhythmical game. The reader will no doubt remember the 'do-re-mi-fa' game, in which we went up and down a four note scale. If we *went on* from do-re-mi-fa we could see that we had three positions.

Do-re-mi-fa, mi-re-do-re, and mi-fa-mi-re and then, corresponding to the twiddle move we can use the reversal move and turn these bars back to front. We then have fa-mi-re-do, re-mi-fa-mi in the order of going on, as it were.

Now it will be seen that, for instance, if we take the note 're' in the first cycle, it occurs either at the second or at the fourth position, yet in the second cycle it occurs either in the first or in the third position. That is, in the first cycle it occurs in even positions, whereas in the second cycle it occurs in odd positions. If we look at the position of 'mi' the same thing will be observed, but, of course, then the 'mi' will be in the odd positions in the first cycle and it will be in the even positions in the second cycle. The same applies to the other notes in each bar, with the proviso that 'do' only occurs in two, not in three, bars and 'fa' only occurs in two, not in three bars. But the odd and even distinction is still preserved. In other words, being odd or even in the position of a particular note in the bar corresponds to the children facing inwards or outwards in the three-cornered waltz. Turning the bar around and singing it backwards corresponds to taking the boy's twiddle and reaching the next position. Going on with the running up and down on our scale, corresponds to taking the left-move for reaching another position.

Do not let us forget that the positions in the dances correspond to the actual bars in the singing or rhythmical game, and it is the changes, that is, the dance steps, that correspond to how you go on from one bar to the next bar, that is, whether you go on with the up and down or whether you change the order of the notes. As we have seen, going on with the up and down corresponds to turning left in the dance and changing the order of the notes for the new bar corresponds to the boy's twiddle.

Figure 89

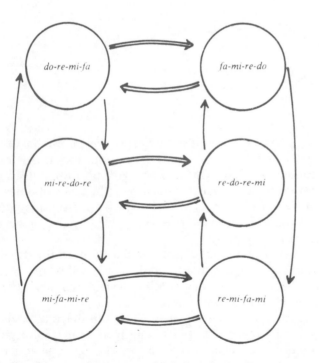

We can easily play another game which has the same structure as this one. Let us get some coasters from the nearest saloon, and collect at least three kinds. We will just call them first, second, and third kinds of coasters. Glasses of beer may be placed on any coaster, as long as two glasses are never placed on neighbouring coasters. This is just to make the game more like a 'saloon' game. We may place the coasters one against the other, so that the circles touch, but so that 'touching' coasters must always be of different kinds. We will soon see that an interesting triangular pattern is created. If we move along a straight line from coaster to coaster, we go through three different coasters in turn until we get back to the first type of coaster. If, on the other hand, we put a glass of beer on one coaster, and go round it, we shall find that we can touch six coasters, one after the other, before we get back to our first coaster.

Figure 90

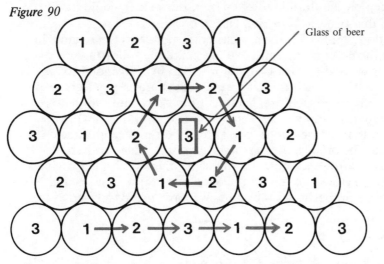

Glass of beer

But we shall see, that we only meet two kinds of coasters on this circular trip because each of them is touching the third kind on which we have placed our glass of beer. Consequently, in this game in a circular tour round the glass of beer, we go from, say, the second kind to the third kind, third to the second, second to the third, and so on, assuming we put our beer on the first kind of coaster. Obviously, we could have put our beer on another kind of coaster, say, the second kind, in which case doing the round of this glass would have exchanged a first kind of coaster for a third kind and a third kind for a first kind.

In what way is this game similar to the do-re-mi-fa's or to the one in which we dance around holding hands? It might be guessed that the three coasters correspond to the three dancers. But how do we get the six positions out of it? Very easy. Take a pencil, for example, and put it down so that one end of the pencil is in one coaster and the other end on another, for instance, pointing from the first kind to the second kind. Let's call such a position of the pencil 'one-two'. If we then advance the pencil one step further so that it now points from the second kind to the third kind of coaster it will then be said to be in position 'two-three'. If we advance it again it will be in position 'three-one', and if we advance it again, it will come back to its position 'one-two', but, of course, three spaces further on. So it needed three advances to bring it from position 'one-two. to a similar position of 'one-two', that is, pointing from the first kind to the second kind of coaster.

We could, of course, still put our beer down on one of the coasters, say, on coaster type one, and then put the pencil near the beer glass, that is, say, pointing from type two or type three. In that case the pencil will be in position 'two-three'. We could then move it around the beer glass so that it goes from 'two-three' to 'three-two', and then 'three-two' to 'two-three', and then 'two-three' to 'three-two' and so on until it comes back to the original 'two-three'. In fact we could go on indefinitely changing from 'two-three' to 'three-two' by letting it go round a particular coaster which we would happen to choose by putting a glass of beer or any other object on it.

We could call this move the 'beer move'. That means that we are always going round the beer glass. That means that 'two-three' goes in to 'three-two', 'three-two' goes in to 'two-three' and so on. But equally, according to the 'beer move', if we happen to have put our beer glass on coaster type two, then it would have taken us from 'one-three' to 'three-one' and from 'three-one' to 'one-three' because our pencil would have been turning around the coaster of the second kind. Or, obviously, if the beer had been on the third kind of coaster, our pencil would have moved from the 'one-two' position to the 'two-one' position and so on.

Now how is all this to do with the do-re-mi-fa? The beer move corresponds to the twiddle in the dance and to the reversal move in the do-re-mi-fa game. We can make the following correspondence: let the do-re-mi-fa correspond to 'one-two', let mi-re-do-re correspond to 'two-three', and let mi-fa-mi-re correspond to 'three-one'. In that case the 'beer move' would lead us from 'one-two' to 'two-one', and since the 'reversal move' leads us from do-re-mi-fa to fa-mi-re-do will be 'two-one'. Correspondingly, re-do-re-mi will be 'three-two' and re-mi-fa-mi will be 'one-three'. And I think it is easily seen that the positions 'one-two', 'two-three', and three-one' will fill in the spaces in the first cycle of the original diagram and 'two-one', 'one-three', and 'three-two' the second row, following the arrows as shown in this same diagram. And changing the order of the figures will allow us to go from one row to the other row. So we have found yet another game which has just the same properties as the games we have already played as we

Figure 91

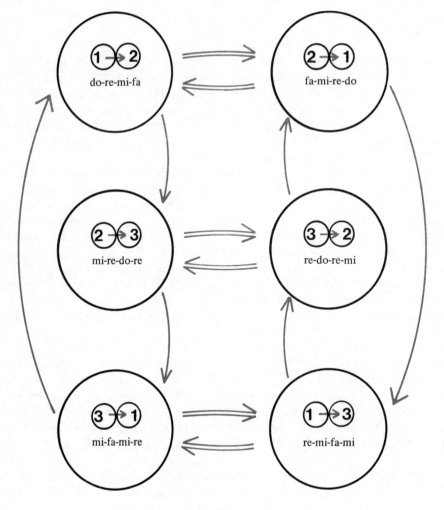

can check by seeing whether what we do in it can be represented by the abstract representation picturing all other games of this kind already played. So this abstract diagram allows us to make the type of discrimination which we have been speaking about earlier.

Somebody might already have wondered what happens if you get four kinds of coasters. Well, there is nothing like trying! Let us see. Put the coasters down in such a way that again no 'touching' coasters should be of the same kind, but let us add another restriction namely that when we have three coasters 'touching', any fourth one which we put against those three has to be the fourth kind and not any one of the three already in the triangle. We shall again get an interesting pattern. Not only must the triangles of coasters be different, but all the diamonds that can be made out of an already constructed triangle by the addition of a fourth coaster must be made of four different kinds of coasters.

Now we can play the pencil game with this arrangement and put a pencil on number one and point it to number two and so on. We now have four different kinds of coasters and every coaster can point towards three other kinds. It is not possible for a coaster to be next to the identical type of coaster. So instead of 16 different kinds of positions we now have 12. Have we already played a game in which there are 12 different kinds of positions? Does this game have the same properties as the ones we might play by pushing our pencil around some more glasses of beer?

Before we think of that let's think of establishing some rules for playing the beer game. For example, we might put a glass of beer down and the pencil down and turn the pencil round the beer glass in a counter-clockwise manner. Or we could turn it in a clockwise manner. It should be noted that in the three coaster game clockwise or counter-clockwise circling around the beer glass would not have made any difference, but we shall see that in this case it does. The reader is referred to fig.92.

Figure 92

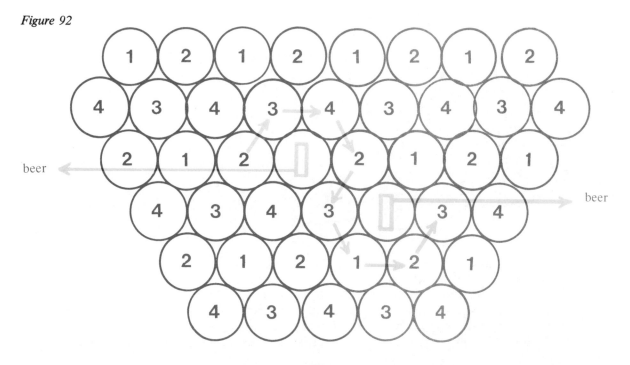

beer

beer

Another game that can be played with coasters is the following. We shall need four coasters, one of each of four different kinds, as well as some sellotape. Tape the four coasters together as shown below:

Figure 93

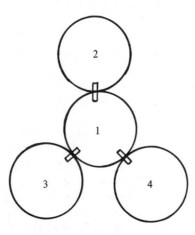

Fold coasters 2, 3 and 4 upwards, while leaving coaster 1 lying horizontally.
Fold them up until they touch.
Tape together the coasters that are now touching.

A pyramid-like object will be obtained with the three sloping coasters 2, 3, 4 forming a kind of enclosing roof. There will be four 'holes' in between the coasters, three next to the 'floor' and one at the top. Looking down from above the pyramid will look like this:

Figure 94

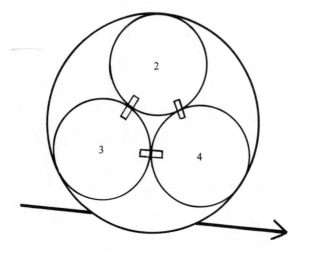

The pyramid or leaky tent may be placed on an arrow so that the arrow touches the point where 3 and 1 meet as well as the point where 4 and 1 meet. One rule of the game is that the arrow always has to touch two such points, that is points where coasters meet.

The position of the tent shown on the figure will be referred to as the position three-four.

The problem now is to find two moves which will enable us to reach all 12 possible positions of the leaky tent. We might choose one move as a right-handed turn (i.e. clockwise) through one third of a whole turn, leaving the coaster that is horizontal in its own plane, in other words leaving it horizontal. This move will do the following shifts:

34 42 23 34 42 etc.

Naturally, we need a move which will 'unseat' the horizontal coaster. We might choose the coaster not touching the arrow and turn it round right-handedly through one third of a whole turn. This will give us, for example,

34 41 13 34 41 etc.

It will be easily verified that all the twelve positions can be reached by using the moves a sufficient number of times in any order of our choosing.

It will also not take long to verify that the pencil and beer game has the same rules as the leaky tent game. The clockwise round the beerglass move corresponds to our first move in the leaky tent game (in which the horizontal coaster stays horizontal); the counter clockwise beerglass move corresponds to our second move in the leaky tent game (in which the coaster not touching the arrow, remains not touching the arrow). Both the games can be 'mapped' on the following diagram:

Figure 95

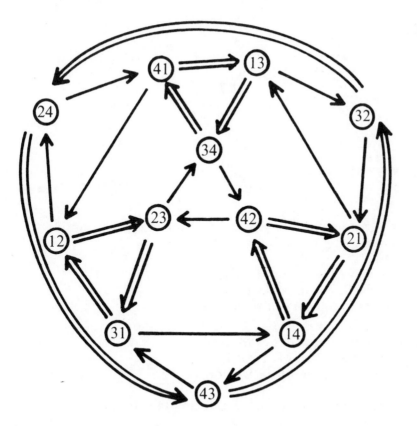

For further games of similar structure, see the author's *Approach to Modern Mathematics.*

Figure 96

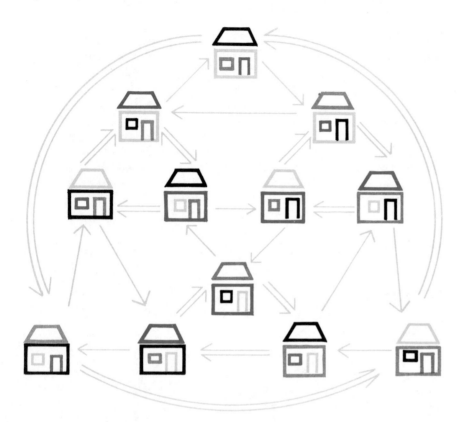

Here is another game which will 'fit' the structure. Just for fun, the diagram is drawn 'upside down'. The rules are obviously as follows:

⟶ : the wall stays the same colour,
    the colour of the window becomes the colour of the roof,
    the colour of the roof becomes the colour of the door,
    the colour of the door becomes the colour of the window.

⟹ : the door stays the same colour,
    the colour of the window becomes the colour of the roof,
    the colour of the roof becomes the colour of the wall,
    the colour of the wall becomes the colour of the window.

It is also possible to make another kind of diagram, by choosing different kinds of moves. For example:

Figure 97

The states of the games of 'moving house' or of 'moving pencils on coasters' are marked, so as to show that both games FIT the same representation. They are therefore the *same kind of game.*

We could play with four kinds of coasters. We can put them out in such a way that in one row from left to right there is a first kind, second kind, first kind, second kind, and so on, and in the next row there is fourth kind, third kind, fourth kind, third kind, fourth kind, third kind, and so on, then we have a triangle four-one-three which has to have a two, that is, a second kind to go with it, so underneath the fourth kind and the third kind there will have to be a second kind. Underneath the third kind and the fourth kind there will have to be a first kind, and so on. So you will have another row of two-one-two-one-two-one, followed by another row of three-four-three-four and so on. In this case, for example, if we put a glass of beer on the first kind of coaster, then we put a pencil pointing from the second kind to the third kind, then we turn to the right, we shall go from the third kind to the fourth kind. Then we turn to the right again, we go from the fourth kind to the second kind. Then we go to the right again, we go from the second kind to the third kind, which is where we started. But if we go to the left from a pencil pointing from the second kind to the third kind, then, of course, we will have to put the glass of beer on the fourth kind of mat. So, if we do this, then we go from the pencil pointing from second to third to a pencil pointing from third to first, then from first to second and then from second to third. So this is quite different going around moving towards the right from moving towards the left. Moving towards the right means of course, a clockwise movement around the beer glass, and moving towards the left means a counter-clockwise movement.

In this chapter we have tried to show how, when a certain stage in abstraction has been reached, that ways of representation can be extremely helpful to gather together that which has been abstracted. This stage, which might be called the fourth stage of the process of learning abstract structures, is largely neglected in the normal learning-teaching situations, except, of course, in real practice where it is necessary. In instruction in industry where types of behaviour have to be learned instead of specific behaviours, many times flow-charts are used, or diagrammatic films presented, to pinpoint the actual relationships that the learner has to look for in applying his skill. Also in industry the learning begins at the practical end and when a number of confrontations have taken place with real practical situations, such as in the workshop, then comparisons between these particular situations take place so that the learner can find out just what he is learning and what kind of principles he can extract from the practice that he has had. In this way he can tackle situations which he has not actually learned in detail, but are of the same kind as the ones he has learned about. It is at this stage that the flow-charts and diagrams are important and only after that is it useful to formulate principles in terms of a technical language.

So in the next chapter we shall try to show what the process can be like when a learner is coming to grips with the fifth stage during which he has to invent or learn a language, and in terms of this language describe the principles that he has extracted through playing, exercises, and diagrammatic activity in the previous stages. So the next stage in the procedure will be one of *symbolization,* whereas the one just described has been one of *representation.*

We shall see later that description is not sufficient, that very often it is not enough to have lengthy and disconnected descriptions of various aspects of what has been learned. The learned material has to be made more systematic and the systematization of the descriptions is what is known in mathematics as *formalization.* Then some of the descriptions which we shall have learned from the diagrams and the general visual pictures will be singled out as the most important. Rules will be determined by means of which other parts of the descriptions can be *deduced.* In this way we construct a much more economical way of describing things. Instead of making all the calculations in a laborious fashion we can provide quick and accurate methods for anybody making such calculations if they so wish. In the case of reasoning, instead of allowing someone merely to describe what he has learned, we can get him to systematize what he has learned so that he can see where all the descriptions fit in with each other. How this is done will be described, then, in a final chapter, and the formalization process will be seen to be the crowning stage in the learning of mathematical concepts.

Any mathematician will agree that a person who is able to handle an axiomatic system, specify the rules of procedure for deduction, and thereby generate theorems in the system knows that part of mathematics. Even more so, if he is able to immediately detect in what practical cases these formally described abstractions are relevant, he has achieved an enviable position in this science. It is not much use knowing a lot of formal mathematics if, when we come across its obvious counter-part in the real world, we do not recognize it. It is no good reading the word 'blue' as b-l-u-e if we do not know a blue chair or a blue motor car when we see one. So, clearly, it is not just the formal language which we need to learn, but all its possible potential links with the real world. It is a great shame that mathematics teaching, particularly at the higher levels, including school, concentrates on the formal level. A great many formal properties are taught and methods of procedure and symbolic languages of various kinds, and then later the student is told in certain particular cases how to apply these symbolic languages to certain practical situations. The result is that when the student comes across a practical application which he has not been taught as being relevant to a certain symbolic language, he does not know this, because he has learned the language before he has learned the situations. We propose to turn the whole thing right round and let the mathematical horse pull the mathematical cart for a change so that we can both have fun finding out things mathematical in the initial stages of learning and then have the satisfaction of being able to categorize and tidy up our knowledge in a very satisfactory and formalized system, which is then much more applicable to general situations then would be the case had we started at the formal end.

7. Mathematical language

Developing a language of precision

IN THE LAST CHAPTER we studied a stage of learning mathematics which we called the 'representational stage'. During this stage we try to put in pictorial or imaged form the abstractions that we have put together out of a large number of varied and different kinds of experiences. We can now assume that when we have this picture before us we are able to empty it of its contents and just regard it as a set of relationships. We are then looking at the picture in order to fix in our minds how certain hypothetical events are related to each other. We must further assume that, given a certain particular set of events, we shall be able to tell whether this set of events does or does not fit the picture. In other words, if we have a number of these pictures, we should know which picture fits which set of events. This is what we call discrimination on a *conceptual level,* as opposed to the kind of discrimination that even animals learn at the *perceptual level.*

But this is by no means the end of the story. Having extracted from the environment this high degree of emptiness and, consequently, a high degree of applicability, we can study the properties of this empty picture. In other words, what have we really found? What does it look like? How does it handle? Although the picture is empty, we shall have to, nevertheless, give its parts some names so that we can talk about them. So the empty spaces where the 'states' of the game used to be, and have now been rubbed out, will be simply called 'mathematical states'. And the ways in which we changed states into other states, that is, the actual events, which have also been rubbed out, will be called 'mathematical operators' or 'functions'. Different operators will be noted by different kinds of letters going from state to state.

In our considerations every operator was able to operate on every state in the game. This is by no means always the case. Take, for example, a subtraction operator like 'subtract two'. This cannot operate on the number 'one' because, if you have a number 'one', it is only possible to subtract 'one' or 'nought' assuming that we are dealing with natural numbers only. So there are some cases where operators will simply not accept certain states on which to operate. These operators will not be able to be applied to some states of mathematical affairs.

In order to describe the properties of the different kinds of functions we may have in particular games, we would need to give these functions some special names. Without names they cannot be described or related to other functions. The states of a game also have to be given certain special names. In arithmetic this is already done for us. The states of the arithmetical game are known as the *cardinal numbers* or as the *counting numbers,* such as zero, one, two, three, four, five, and so on. The usual arithmetical functions are adding, subtracting, multiplying, and dividing. So we could go quite a long way in describing some of the properties of our arithmetical games if we developed some suitable and precise language in terms of which these properties can be explained and described.

The language of arithmetic

Arithmetic abounds in many different kinds of operations. Let us choose multiplication as our example, for showing how a language may be developed. The 'states' in our game will be numerical states. The 'multipliers' will be operators which turn each element in a state into several elements of another state as though by magic. For example, one such operator might be 'put four elements for each one'. Of course, this is not *really* magic because we are not 'creating' four actual objects every time we have one object in a state. We can put four of one kind of object somewhere everytime there is one of a certain other kind of object present. For example, we may have a number of tables in a cafe and we might decide to put four chairs around each table. So the number of chairs will be obtained by *multiplying* the number of tables by four. So the operator, at the concrete level, will be: 'let us have four chairs around each table'. At the abstract level the operator will be 'take four for one', or, even more simply, 'multiply by four'. So any state can be multiplied by a multiplier operator and another state can thus be obtained. If there are three tables, there will be twelve chairs. If there are four tables, there will be 16 chairs, and so on.

The operator transforms each state into some other state of the same game. The schematic representation of this would be to write '3' in an empty space and then have an arrow in which one could put 'multiply by 4', deciding that an arrow of a certain colour will always mean a multiplication by 4. Or we could put a little '4' on the arrow to distinguish it from other arrows which may be multiplications by other numbers. And at the head of this arrow we shall have to put the figure '12'.

Now, of course, from the state '3' we shall be able to move away with other operators, not just by 'multiply by 4'. For example, another arrow can leave, on which we write '2 times', or 'multiply by 2', and this will lead to the state '6'. Now, from the state '6', again, another arrow can leave which is also, say, a 'multiplication by 2', and this will arrive at the same state as the state at which we arrived before. In other words, we can go from '3' to '12' in two ways. We can go from '3' to '6' by a '2 timesing' arrow and from '6' to '12' by another '2 timesing' arrow. And from '3' to '12' we can go directly by a '4 timesing' arrow. This triangle joining 3, 6 and 12 has the three sides,

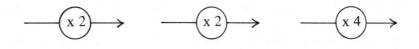

We can go from ③ to ⑫ , directly or via ⑥ . This triangle can be used not only for the state ③ but for any other state from which the 'four timesing' and the 'two timesing' arrows start.

Figure 98

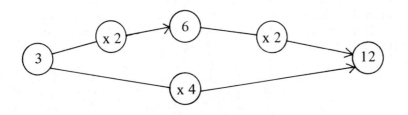

Symbolically, we can say

$$\left[3 \left(x\,2 \right) \right] \left(x\,2 \right) = 3 \left(x\,4 \right)$$

For instance, if we start with the state $\left(4 \right)$, the '4 timesing' arrow

Figure 99

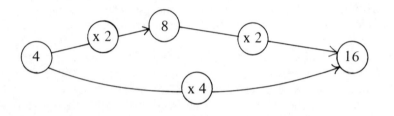

Symbolically,

$$\left[4 \left(x\,2 \right) \right] \left(x\,2 \right) = 4 \left(x\,4 \right)$$

It will be easy to see that the succession of two '2 timesers' will always give us a '4 timeser' quite independently of where we start and where we finish. As long as we start at the same state we shall finish up at the same state if we take a '2 timeser' followed by another '2 timeser' or if we take a '4 timeser'. How we express this in mathematics by saying that '4 timesing' comes to the same thing as '2 timesing' followed by another '2 timesing' 'Coming to the same thing' in mathematics is called 'being equivalent'. So we can say in arithmetical language that

We could, of course, find many other ways of getting from 3 to 12 , or 4 to 16 . For example, we could take an '8 timeser' which would take us to 24 and then we could say that when you have got the 24 , every time you see two things you are to replace them with one thing. That will lead us to the 12 . For example, we might say that we have three children and each child gets eight pencils. But then each set of two pencils has to be put say in a box. So that means we have three children, and eight pencils for one child leads us to the 24 pencils, but one box for two pencils tells us that we need the 12 boxes.

Figure 100

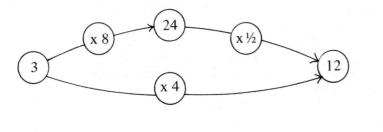

Symbolically,

$$\left[3 \left(\text{x } 8\right)\right] \left(\text{x } \tfrac{1}{2}\right) = 3 \left(\text{x } 4\right)$$

So, symbolically, we have still reached the number ⑫, starting from the number ③, by taking an '8 timesing', following by a 'Halving'. We can also soon convince ourselves that an '8 timeser' followed by a 'halver' will always come to the same thing as a '4 timeser'. In arithmetical language

$$\left(\text{x } 8\right) \left(\text{x } \tfrac{1}{2}\right) \equiv \left(\text{x } 4\right)$$

There are an infinite number of ways in which we could go from place to place each of which could be equivalent to the first way that we have taken. Let us go on to the description we would need, to give an account of these various equivalences. The fact that a '2 timeser' and a '2 timeser' is equivalent to a '4 timeser' can be written down as one of the properties of the game. This corresponds to the fact that twice two are four. So we might not be surprised to find that if we double a certain number and then we treble what we have doubled, we have in fact multiplied our number by six. This corresponds to two times three being six. So in this way we could regard our 'timesing' machines as objects which can be put together by putting them end to end. And this putting together would seem to correspond to what in ordinary arithmetic is called multiplication. For this reason we could call them the 'products' and even use the letter P to show that we have thus put them together. For example, we could write P ('2 timeser' '3 timeser') = '6 timeser'. In the same way the product of a 2 timeser' and a '2 timeser' will be a '4 timeser' or P ('2 timeser' '2 timeser') = '4 timeser' or abbreviating even more we could write simply P 2, 2 = 4. The word or numeral '4', in this case, already means a '4 timeser' not just a '4'. Similarly, we could say that P 2, 3 = 6, which means that a '2 timeser' followed by a '3 timeser' is equivalent to a '6 timeser', or we could say, diagrammatically speaking, that the following two 'machines' are equivalent:

Figure 101

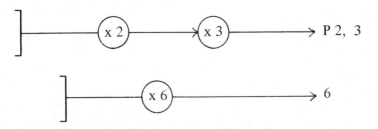

Now, what about adding two multiplying operators? What does that mean? Well, we can multiply a number by two and we can multiply that same number by three and add the results. But, as everybody knows, we will have multiplied our number by five and not by six. This operation can be denoted by S (for 'sum of', you will recall). So, when we add the results of two multiplying operators applied to the same number, the operator which does the same work as this combined operator is the one we obtain when we multiply by the sum of the two multipliers. This is seen in the diagram below, where it is clear that 5 is also a binary operator, whose arguments are the unary operators themselves namely,

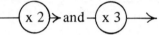

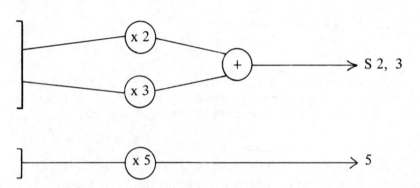

It will perhaps be appreciated that the first way of combining multiplying operators is a version of the associative law of multiplication. Let us take an input 1 and multiply this by 2. We shall have 1 times 2. This is the output of the first part of the chain. If we then multiply this output by 3, we shall have (1 times 2) times 3. On the other hand, everybody knows that this could have been obtained by 1 being multiplied by 6, that is by (2 times 3). In other words, 1 times (2 times 3) is the same as (1 times 2) times 3 and this is the classical associative principle of multiplication.

Figure 103

I ⊢ —(x 2)— 1 x 2 —→(x 3)—→ (I x 2) x 3

I ⊢ —(x 6)—→ I x 6 = I x (2 x 3)

On the other hand, if we take an input and multiply it by 2, we shall have 4 times 2. If we take the same input and multiply it by 3, we shall have 4 times 3. Adding these outputs, we shall have (4 times 2) plus (4 times 3), which is equal to 4 times 5, or, in other words, 4 times (2 plus 3). We shall no doubt recognize the distributive law. So, when we are dealing with given inputs, and using the end-on method of combining multiplying operators, we are making use of the associative law. That is, we replace the chain of these two operators by the one operator to which the chain is equivalent. On the other hand, when we are using a given input, and applying to this input two different multiplying operators, and the two results thus obtained are added, we have a different situation. That is, we are looking for the single multiplying operator which is equivalent to the two multiplying operators used 'side by side'. We are making use of the distributive principle as applied to states and operators.

Figure 104

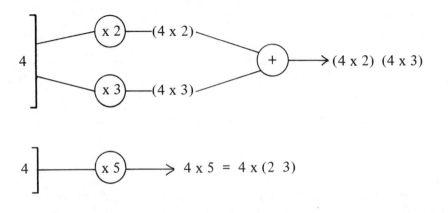

The associative and the distributive principles look somewhat different when applied to operators only, as we shall see.

Successive applications of the P and the S functions

We now develop the notation for combinations of sums and products of multiplying operators and combine them, after which we could place at the output end of this chain a sum of two multiplying operators. In other words, we could put an operator such as P 2, 3 end-on with an operator such as S 2, 3. The P 2, 3 will be a 'doubler' followed by a 'tripler' along a single channel. At the output end of the 'tripler' there will be two channels emanating, one going into a 'doubler' and the other going, let us say, below it, into a 'tripler'. The outputs of these will be led into an adding operator, a binary adding operator to be more specific, which will produce the final output. So, here we have a P 2, 3 end-on with an S 2, 3 and, therefore, the way to symbolize it would be P P 2, 3 S 2, 3.

Figure 105

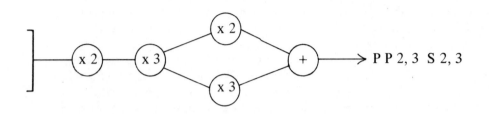

Naturally, we can have simpler ways of combining P's and S's (products and sums) of multiplying operators. For example, let us see what P S 2, 3, 4 looks like. Read out as an English sentence, it says: The product of the sum of a 'doubler' and a 'tripler' with a 'quadrupler'. So, at the input end, we shall start off with two channels, one leading to a 'doubler' and one to a 'tripler'.

Figure 106

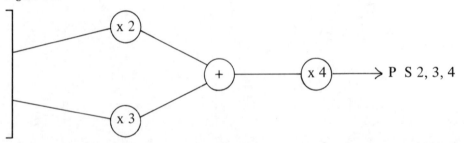

The outputs of these two channels will be joined together into an 'adder' and the output from the 'adder' will lead into a 'quadrupler'. The output from this 'quadrupler' is the output of the whole chain of operators. The children who play games with these chains of operators like to call them machines. So, this is a P S 2, 3, 4 machine. But what do we get with a slight switch in notation, say, an S P 2, 3, 4 machine? This is the sum of the product of a 'doubler' and a 'tripler' with a 'quadrupler'. Being a sum, it has to have two channels which lead to an 'adder' at the end of the machine. But what is this the sum of? It is the sum of a product of a 'doubler' with a 'tripler', added to a 'quadrupler'. So, the upper channel from the input end will start with a 'doubler' followed by a 'tripler'. The lower channel will lead into a 'quadrupler' and the output of these two chains will be brought together in an 'adder' which will disgorge the total output at the very end of the machine.

Figure 107

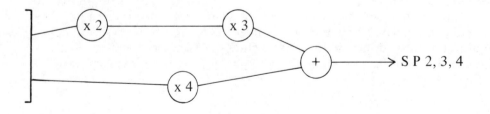

We can have products of sums, or sums of products, if we want to have things more complicated. For example, what would be the S of P 2, 3 and P 3, 4? Since it is an S, it must have two channels, an upper channel and a lower channel, which will lead into an adding machine which will further lead into the output. So, the S of P 2, 3 and P 3, 4 will have an upper channel which consists of a 'doubler' followed by a 'tripler'. It will also have a lower channel which starts with a 'tripler' and leads into a 'quadrupler'. The output of the 'doubler-tripler' channel will meet the output of the 'tripler-quadrupler' channel at the adding machine which will disgorge the final output.

Figure 108

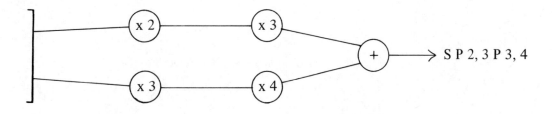

S P 2, 3 P 3, 4

Now, what is the product of the two sums? What is, for example, P S 2, 3 S 3, 4? As we have indicated, P means putting end-on, end-to-end, or one after the other. Therefore, P of S 2, 3 and S 3, 4 is the end-on positioning of the sum of a 'doubler' with a 'tripler', along with the sum of a 'tripler' and a 'quadrupler'. So, from the first input, we shall have an upper channel which has just one 'doubler' in it and a lower channel which has just one 'tripler' in it. These will lead into an adding machine, leading again into an output. This output then will split again into two channels, an upper one and a lower one. The upper one will be the 'tripler' and the lower one will lead into a 'quadrupler'. These again will come together in an adding machine, a binary adding machine, to be specific. From this adding machine will disgorge the total output of this machine.

Figure 109

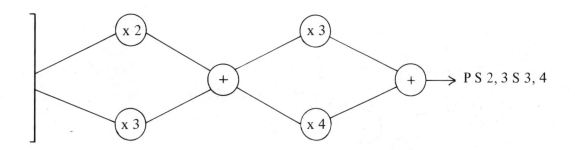

P S 2, 3 S 3, 4

The associative principle of addition

Let us take S S 2, 3, 4. This is the sum of the sum of a 'doubler' and a 'tripler' with a 'quadrupler'. In other words, the input has three channels. The first channel goes into a 'doubler', the second channel into a 'tripler', and their outputs go as inputs into an 'adder' which produces its own output. The third channel leads into a 'quadrupler'. The output of this 'quadrupler' and the output of the previous 'adder' come together in another 'adder'. It is the output of this final 'adder' which is the output of the whole machine. So, we have taken the sum of a 'doubler' and a 'tripler' and added it to a 'quadrupler'. This is the meaning of S S 2, 3, 4 because we are 'S-ing' the S 2, 3 with the 4.

Figure 110

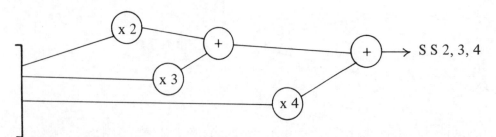

Now, we could just as well have taken the S of the 2 and the S 3, 4 and, by the associative principle, we should have had an equivalent machine. In other words, we could have taken the first channel which would have let into a 'doubler', then the second and the third channels, which would have, in turn, let into a 'tripler' and a 'quadrupler'. But the outputs of these last two would then lead into an 'adder', the output of which would join the output of the first channel in yet another 'adder', which would produce the output of the whole machine. In this way, we can see that S S 2, 3, 4 is equivalent to S 2 S 3, 4. The sum of the sum of a 'doubler' and a 'tripler' with a 'quadrupler' is an equivalent machine to one that combines the sum of a 'doubler' with the sum of a 'tripler' and a 'quadrupler'. Formally, all that happens is that the second S and the 2 are interchanged.

Figure 111

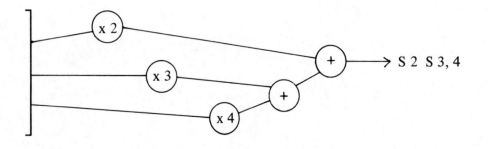

This principle does not only apply to simple machines. Instead of the machines 'doubler' and 'tripler' and 'quadrupler', we could have used any other machines of a multiplying character, and put them together in this way. Let these machines be symbolized by □, △, ◇. Then we can say that:

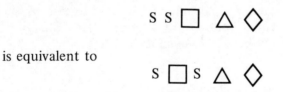

S S □ △ ◇

is equivalent to

S □ S △ ◇

This is the symbolic form of expressing the general version of the associative principle for addition in the new notation suggested.

Figure 112

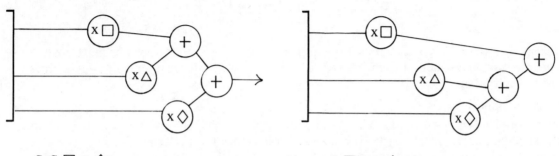

S S □△◇   S □S △ ◇

Commutativity of addition

Further, for additions it does not matter which is the upper channel and which is the lower channel. This can be stated by saying:

Figure 113

S □ △ is equivalent to S △□ or diagrammatically

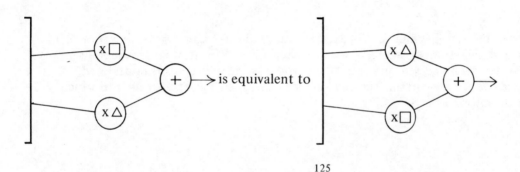

is equivalent to

Associativity of multiplication

It is almost trivially obvious that P P 2, 3, 4 is equivalent to P 2 P 3, 4. In our case this means that the putting together, one after the other of a 'doubler' and a 'tripler' followed by a 'quadrupler' will give us exactly the machine which we would obtain if we took a 'doubler' at the end of which we put a 'tripler' and a 'quadrupler' joined end-to-end. In each case, we would get a 'doubler' followed by a 'tripler' followed by a 'quadrupler'. This, of course, applies equally to any machines which can be symbolized by a □ △ and ◇.
So, we can state that:

$$P \ P \ \square \ \triangle \ \diamond \quad \text{is equivalent to} \quad P \ \square \ P \triangle \diamond$$

Commutativity of multiplication

It is equally obvious that the commutative principle holds for the P operator. We can symbolize this by saying:

$$P \ \square \triangle \quad \text{is replaceable by} \quad P \ \triangle \square$$

This means that when we put two multiplying operators end-to-end, it does not matter which of them we put first and which of them second. In each case we shall get operators or machines equivalent to each other.

The neutral multiplier

Among the multiplying operators, there is one special operator which produces 1 at the output for each 1 at the input. In other words, it is a neutral operator or a 'multiplier by 1'.

We know that if we place end-to-end the neutral operator with any other this chain is equivalent to this other operator. This can be symbolized by saying

$$P \ 1 \ \square \quad \text{can be replaced by} \quad \square; \quad \text{diagrammatically}$$

Figure 114

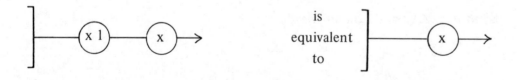

In fact, if we have any set of symbols, proceded by a P 1, that P 1 can simply be left out. Or, if we have any meaningful string of symbols, we can place a P 1 in front of it. This merely means that we are placing a neutral operator in front of the whole string of operators considered. Clearly, by doing so, we are not altering the equivalence class of strings of operators to which our first string of operators belongs.

The distributive principle

So, we have dealt with the associative principle, the commutative principle, and the principle of the neutral with the P operator or multiplication. We have also dealt with the commutative and the associative principles as far as the S operator, or addition, *is concerned.* We could introduce a neutral element for addition, which would be 0, i.e. the operator of taking '0 for 1'.

It must be remembered, that in this game, there is no such thing as adding 2 or adding 3. Addition is a binary operator. Each element of the game is itself a multiplier which multiplies something whereby we obtain something else. The elements are the operators themselves! When we multiply, so to speak, two operators, we in fact put them end-to-end, that is, in series. When we add two operators, we put them in parallel.

Let us now consider the distributive principle, *the principle being the link between the P operator and the S operator.* In other words, it tells us in what way putting operators in parallel and putting operators in series can be linked with each other and how they can be transformed so as not to leave the equivalence class to which a given string of operators belongs.

Let us take, for example, the sum of two products. Consider the sum of the product of a 'doubler' with a 'tripler', with the product of a 'quadrupler' with a 'tripler'. In other words we are considering two channels leading to an 'adder' at the end of the machine. The first channel emanating from the input will contain a 'doubler' followed by a 'tripler'. The second channel will contain a 'quadrupler' followed by a 'tripler'. Their outputs will lead into an 'adder' which will then lead to the final output.

Figure 115

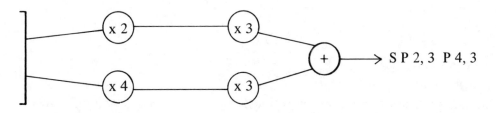

This is, therefore, an S P 2, 3, P 4, 3. It will not take long for children to discover that such a machine is equivalent to one which we construct in the following way: take the input and in the first channel take a 'doubler'. In the second channel, take a 'quadrupler'. Lead the outputs of these two into an 'adder' and lead the output of the 'adder' into a 'tripler' whose output will be the output of the entire machine. In our terminology, this will be the product of the sum of the 'doubler' and the 'quadrupler' by the 'tripler'.

Figure 116

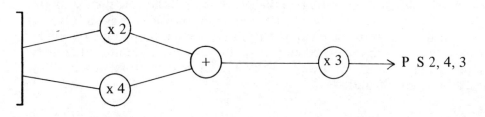

In other words, this will be P S 2, 4, 3 because we are putting end-to-end the sum of the 'doubler' and 'quadrupler' with a 'tripler'.

It will be seen that this is not just a particular case but it is quite general. In other words, if we take again □ , △ and ◇ , as symbols for general multiplicative operators, we have the following equivalence statements which we can make: the machine whose input leads into the first channel with a □ followed by a ◇ and at the same time into the second channel with a △ followed by a ◇ , the outputs of the two ◇ 's will lead into an 'adder' whose output is the total output of the machine. The above machine is equivalent to the following: the input has, again, two channels. The first channel leads into a □ and the second into a △ ; the outputs of these two lead into an 'adder' whose output leads into a ◇ , whose output is the total output of the machine. In other words, in our symbolic way of writing, we can write:

Figure 117

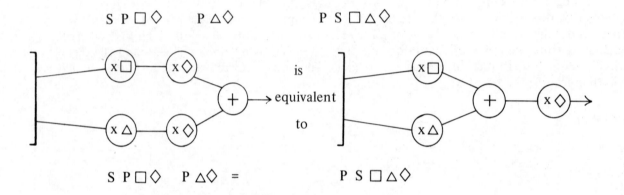

$$S\ P\ \square\ \diamond \quad P\ \triangle\diamond\ =\quad\quad\quad P\ S\ \square\ \triangle\diamond$$

Link with the conventional notation

If we wish to tie this new notation in with the conventional notation, we can do so quite easily. Let us take, for example, to make matters easier, machines which proceed from right to left. This is because, in most manuals, the multiplier in x times y is considered to be x and the multiplicand is considered to be the y. In other words, y is the input, x is the multiplier, and x times y is the output. For this reason it is better to have the input on the right, the machine in the middle, and the output on the left. Let us accept the normal convention, that when there is more than one operation to be performed, those operations to be done first are enclosed in parentheses.

Let us take the distributive law first. Let us say that x stands for the input and that we have a 'doubler' on the upper channel and a 'tripler' on the lower channel. Then the output of these will be respectively 2x and 3x. The 2 will be written on the left of the x, following the fact that the 'doubler' is on the left of the input x. The 3 will be written on the left of x, as again it is easily seen that the 'tripler' is on the left of the input x. These two channels now come together in an 'adder'. When we have an 'adder' in the conventional notation, we must put down the first input and the second input with a plus sign in between. This will represent our total output. In this case, we shall have 2x plus 3x as the output.

Figure 118

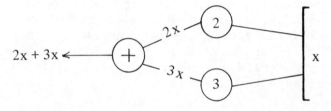

To be exact, we really should have made a multiplication sign between the 2 and the x as well as between the 3 and the x. We should also have put the 2 times x in parentheses and the 3 times x in parentheses because those are the operations which have to be performed first. We can, no doubt, adopt the usual conventions that if there are no parentheses, then the multiplications are performed first. All these conventions are, of course, not necessary if you use either the network or machine system as shown above, or the system of notation with Ps and Ss. But there is no reason why the two notations should not run side by side, or why one should not lead to the other, or vice versa.

Let us now take the two multiplying operators applied one after the other. Let us take a 'doubler' followed by a 'tripler'. If x is the input, 2x will be the output which goes into the tripling machine. So, 3 times (2x) will be the output of the 'two times' followed by the 'three times' machine.

Figure 119

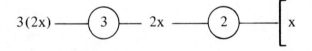

We know, of course, by the properties of numbers, that this number is bound to be the same as 6 times x that is (3 times 2) times x.

Let us go back to the 'parallel' or adding machine. When we are dealing with such a two-channel or adding situation, there naturally is no need to make the restriction that at the input end the 'doubler' and the 'tripler' must have the same inputs. One could be x and the other could be y. In this case the output would be symbolized by 2x plus 3y, for example:

Figure 120

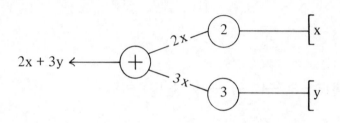

The conventional algebraic symbolism would then describe the state of affairs at the output and and the new algebraic symbolism would describe the way in which the operators have been put together in order to achieve the result at the end. So-called simplifications would then be carried out through a knowledge of the workings of the equivalence classes of chains of operators. We would know, for example, that P 3 P 4, 5 can be replaced by P P 3, 4, 5 in virtue of the associative principle for putting operators end-to-end, that P 3, 4 can be replaced by P 4, 3 by the commutative principle for end-to-ending, and so on.

The beginnings of a formal system

We have established *inductively* that the following equivalences hold in our system, whose elements are *unary multiplying operators:*

(C_s) $\quad$ S $\square$ $\triangle$ $\quad$ = $\quad$ S $\triangle$ $\square$ $\qquad$ (C_p) $\quad$ P $\square$ $\triangle$ $\qquad$ = $\quad$ P $\triangle$ $\square$

(A_s) $\quad$ S S $\square$ $\triangle$ $\diamondsuit$ $\quad$ = S $\square$ S$\triangle$$\diamondsuit$ $\qquad$ (A_p) $\quad$ P P $\square$ $\triangle$ $\diamondsuit$ $\quad$ = P $\square$ P$\triangle$$\diamondsuit$

(N_s) $\quad$ S O $\square$ $\quad$ = $\quad$ $\square$ $\qquad\qquad$ (N_p) $\quad$ P 1 $\square$ $\qquad$ = $\quad$ $\square$

$\qquad\qquad$ (D) P S $\square$$\triangle$$\diamondsuit$ $\qquad\qquad$ = $\qquad\qquad$ S P $\square$$\diamondsuit$ P$\triangle$$\diamondsuit$

To be more specific, we could include some more *special* equivalences, such as

Figure 121

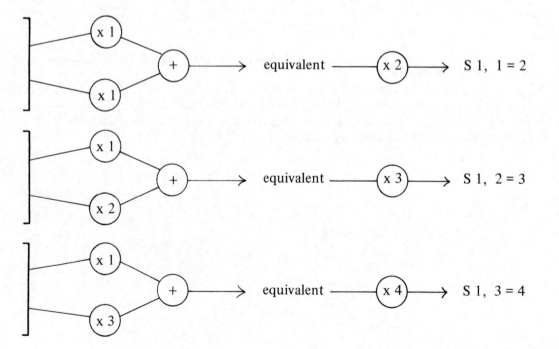

Let us now see how we can carry our so-called simplifications, assuming only the above listed equivalences. For example, we know from practice that a machine which consists of a 'doubler' followed by a 'tripler', is equivalent to a machine which is the sum of a 'tripler' with another 'tripler'. We may ask whether we have enough information already, in terms of which we can now *deduce* that this must be so? In other words, is the new information already contained in the information given by the list?

We wish to show that

Figure 122

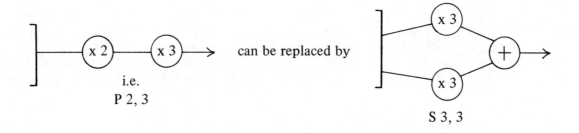

i.e.
P 2, 3

can be replaced by

S 3, 3

Let us start with

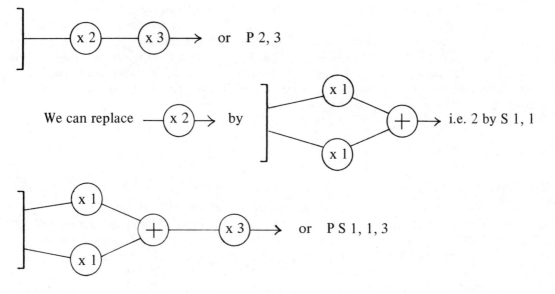

or   P 2, 3

We can replace ──(x 2)→ by   i.e. 2 by S 1, 1

or   P S 1, 1, 3

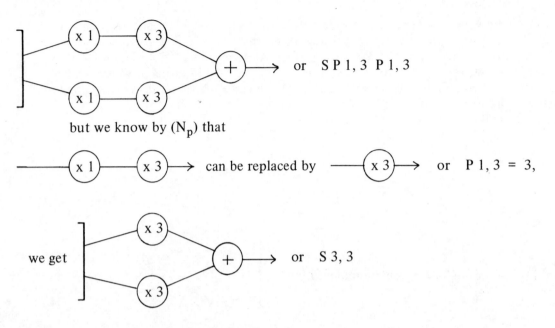

but we know by (N_p) that

we get

or S 3, 3

We will find that this is, in fact, the case.

We have now proved our first theorem which states:
$$P\ 2, 3 = S\ 3, 3.$$

We can also prove simple theorems such as S 2, 2 equals 4. This means that a 'doubler' in parallel with another 'doubler' is equivalent to a 'quadrupler'. This is obviously true, but can we prove it? Again, the first 2 in the S 2, 2 can be replaced by an S 1, 1 so we have S S 1, 1, 2. Now by the associative principle, the second S and the first 1 can be interchanged so that we have S 1 S 1, 2. But we have just seen that S 1, 2 can be replaced by 3, so that we have S 1, 3. Since we have seen that S 1, 3 can be replaced by 4, we have, through admissible operations, replaced S 2, 2 by 4. In this case, we have had to use the associative law. In the previous proof, we relied on the distributive law.

And all this without the headaches of any brackets!

The multiplicative inverse

We can go a little further into the game by introducing the inverses of the multiplying operators. A 'three times-er' takes 3 at the output for every 1 at the input. The inverse operator of this would be one that would take 1 at the output for every 3 at the input. We can see straight away that such inverse operators cannot accept every input if such inputs are represented by the cardinal numbers of certain sets of objects. But we can still speak of equivalence of one chain of operators to another chain of operators by simply makings this qualification: in deciding whether one chain is equivalent to another, we consider only those inputs which are acceptable by both chains. With this restriction, we can go on combining inverses of operators with operators, and so on. So, for example, the inverse of a 'three times-er' followed by a 'three times-er' is equivalent to a 'one times-er'.

Figure 123

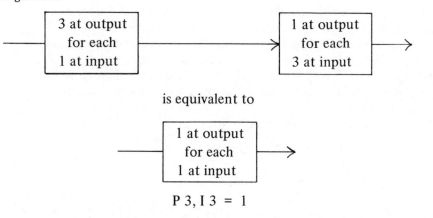

is equivalent to

P 3, I 3 = 1

We need a notation for the inverse. We could use a capital I. A capital I written before the formula symbolizing an operator will then symbolize the inverse of that operator. The digit 3 represents a 'three times-er' so I 3 will represent a 'one for three-er', that is 1 at the output for 3 at the input. So, if we wish to say that the product of the 'one-for-three' by a 'three-for-one' is equivalent to a 'one-for-one', we would have to say P I 3, 3 is equivalent to 1.

In effect, if □ indicates any operator, we shall know that

P I □ □ is always equivalent to 1,

where 1 is the neutral operator. This is another axiom which completes the system of axioms which we need for developing all the theorems necessary for multiplications and divisions of the rational numbers. For instance, we can represent 'taking the two thirds of' as an operator, by P 2 I 3 or else P I 3, 2 because we will have, in effect, taken 2 at the final output for 3 at the initial input. So, if we take 2 at the output for 3 at the input, we are obviously taking two-thirds of the input to obtain the output. So, in this way, we can now introduce the whole calculus of of multiplication and division of fractions. We can now begin to prove things like

Figure 124

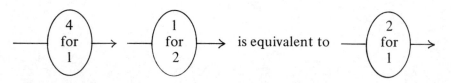

Symbolically written, P 4, I 2 = 2. We need to find a series of allowed replacements to lead us to 2, that is, to a 'doubler' starting from P 4, I 2 or

Figure 125

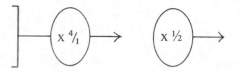

to show that a 'quadrupler' followed by a 'halfer' is equivalent to a 'doubler'. One way of doing this would be to replace 4 by S 2, 2, which we have already proved, so that P 4, I 2 becomes P S 2, 2 I 2. Now we know that P S 2, 2 I 2 by the distributive law can be replaced by S P 2 I 2 P 2 I 2. By the commutative law, P 2 I 2 can be replaced by P I 2, 2. So now the whole string can be replaced by S P I 2, 2 P I 2, 2. We know by the properties of the inverses that P I 2, 2 = 1. So, the first P I 2, 2 can be replaced by 1, and the second P I 2, 2 also by 1. Therefore the whole string is replaced by S 1, 1, which, as we know, can be replaced by 2. So, we have again performed a proof following from our axioms.

The 'proof' would look like this, when put in diagrammatic form

Figure 126

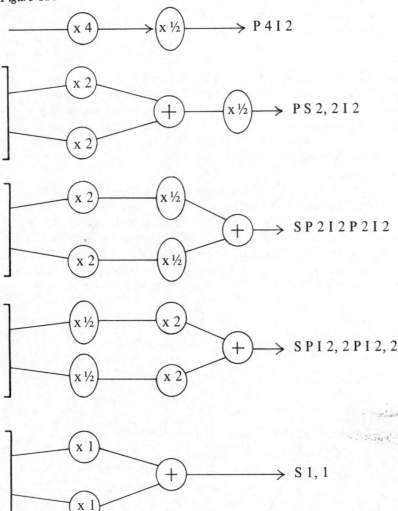

An interesting exercise for the reader would be to show that I P □ △ , can always be replaced by P I □ , I △ , that is, the inverse of the product is the product of the inverses. Having proved that, he should have no difficulty in carrying out various other simplifications in situations where the factoring of a denominator needs to take place.

It will be seen that we have introduced adding, multiplying and dividing. We have not introduced subtracting. There are certain difficulties in the way of this, but there are solutions of a somewhat different type than those discussed in this paper, but following a similar technique.

Construction of another language

Let us now develop some languages for some of the other games and see in what way these languages are different from the language just developed and in what way they are similar to it. If we can find some common features of *all these mathematical languages,* such affinity between the languages might help us to learn other mathematical languages, should the need arise. It is always better to concentrate on learning how to learn something rather than on learning particular things. So we would not like to leave the reader at the point where he is shown ways of developing one particular language. It would be more achievement to learn something about *how to construct such languages.*

Let us take the three-cornered waltz or the triangle game as our first example. Here we have six different states, so it should not be difficult simply to call these six different names. Since we do not want to refer to either the dance or the six-district town or any of the rhythm games, we shall have to invent six rather neutral sounding names for our states, which can at any time be replaced by the particular names of the particular games in any application we wish to make of whatever it is we are able to do with our language.

Let us call the states a, b, c, x, y, z. It will be remembered that there is a move in this kind of a game which creates cycles of three. Let one of these moves turn a into b, b into c and then c back into a whereas it will turn z into y, y into x and x back into z. This move might correspond to a 'go to your left' in the dance. In the moving game it might mean 'paint your door the colour of your window, paint your window the colour of your wall, and paint your wall the colour of your door', or some such move that we like to think up in any particular game of this game structure.

We need to have a name for such a move. We could choose the letter r. Now, of course, to every one of these three-cycles, there is always an opposite three-cycle. Let us call the cycle opposite to r the cycle s. The cycles r and s being opposite to one another, we have the situation where if we change a state by the move r and then we apply s to the resulting state, we shall obtain the original state at which we started. This leads us to the necessity of having a name for starting from the state and getting back to the same state, in other words, for doing nothing. The usual symbol for this is either a 'O' or '1'. A zero is used if the operation which we use on our states is going to be likened to addition, and one is used if this operation is going to be likened to multiplication. Since we are going to put these moves end to end very shortly, we are going to use '1', because we have seen that in the multiplying game putting operators end to end can be likened to a multiplication.

So we now have three moves, 1, r and s. l is 'you stay where you are', r is 'do the cycle in one way', and s, 'do the cycle the other way'. Do not let us forget that doing r takes a to b, and b to c, and c to a but takes x to z and z to y and y to x, whereas the cycle s takes a to c, and c to b, and b to a but takes x to y and y to z and z to x.

Now, in the six-move game, we shall remember that there are three exchanging moves which exchange states for each other, so that by exchanging them again we reach our original state. We shall need three more symbols for these moves. Well, we could say that if a and x are interchanged, or b and y are interchanged, and c and z are interchanged, the move would be called u. On the other hand, if a and y are interchanged, b and z are interchanged, and c and x are interchanged, the move would be called v. On the other hand, if a and z are interchanged, b and x are interchanged, and c and y are interchanged, the move would be called w.

In the three-cornered waltz the 1 would be interpreted by dancing round a circle and coming back to the same position, r could be interpreted as the left move, and s as the right move, or the other way around. The moves u, v, w are the various twiddle moves by means of which we change from facing inside to facing outside, or, of course, from facing outside to facing inside.

But we are not at all at home yet in this 'describing game', because we have no symbol for 'putting an operator behind another operator'. We used such 'putting end to end' in the multiplying game, and we used the letter P for symbolizing this act. There is no reason why we should not use P here as well. So P will mean that we apply the operator written next to the letter P first, followed by the operator which is written next. In other words 'P' means 'join the two operators together, first the first and the second next'. For example, we could state that P r s = 1 because, under all circumstances, if we apply r and then s, we shall have come back to the original starting point. This is how s was constructed as being 'just the opposite' of r. So the 'product' of the r move by the s move is equivalent to the 1 move, or, the 'doing nothing' move. We use the equal sign ' = ' for the equivalence relation, which means 'comes to the same thing as'. So we could now write down 36 different equivalences. For instance, we could write that P r r = s, P r u = v and so on.

Below is the whole multiplication table of the elements 1, r, s, u, v, and w of the game that we have now symbolized:

Figure 127

P 1 1 = 1	P 1 r = r	P 1 s = s	P 1 u = u	P 1 v = v	P 1 w = w
P r 1 = r	P r r = s	P r s = 1	P r u = v	P r v = w	P r w = u
P s 1 = s	P s r = 1	P s s = r	P s u = w	P s v = u	P s w = v
P u 1 = u	P u r = w	P u s = v	P u u = 1	P u v = s	P u w = r
P v 1 = v	P v r = u	P v s = w	P v u = r	P v v = 1	P v w = s
P w 1 = w	P w r = v	P w s = u	P w u = s	P w v = r	P w w = 1

Generators

If we look at the above table, we may find of interest that, for example, v and w, as well as s, could be expressed in terms of r and u only; s can be expressed as P r r, v can be expressed as P r u, w can be expressed P u r. This means that u and r are sufficient for *generating* all the elements in the game. Naturally, s and u would have done just as well, or r and v, or r and w, or else s and v, or s and w. Even u and v would have done as we can see that u followed by v is s, whereas v followed by u is r. Likewise w can be expressed as P P v u v. We can see that any two

Figure 128

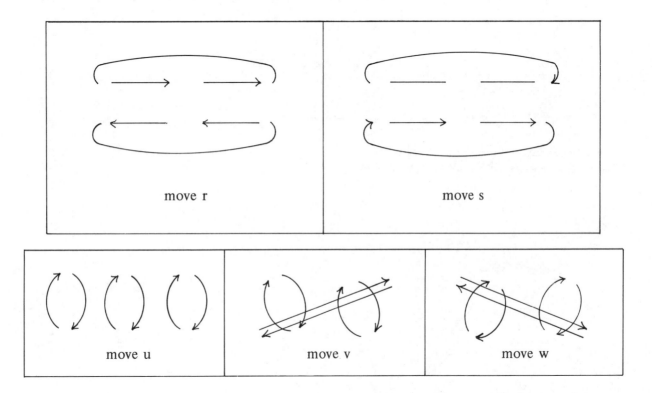

move r

move s

move u

move v

move w

of the three elements u, v, and w will do to describe the rest, or any one of the two elements r, s with any one of the three elements u, v, w will likewise do to describe all the rest. This can be made clearer by just looking at the diagrams below. These are the diagrams that help us to reach a stage four type of representation. The description of these diagrams is what we are now attempting to carry out.

Figure 129

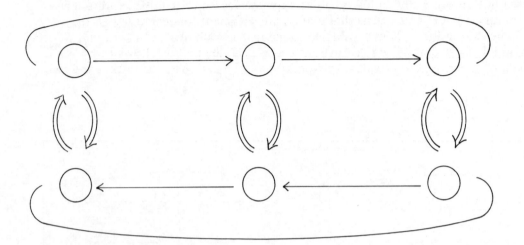

For ⟹ we can choose r or s
For ⟹ we can choose u, v or w

Figure 130

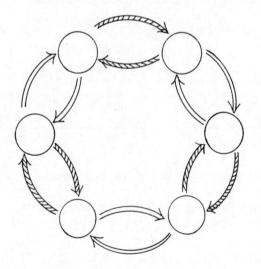

For ⟹ we can choose u, v, or w.
For ⟹ we can choose u, v, or w but not one we have
already chosen for ⟹

Let us go back to the 36 equivalences whose table we gave a little while back. There is an enormous amount of redundant information there. It is possible to give this information in a more restricted form, in a more economical form, so that from it somebody can deduce all the rest. We suggest the following: The product of the product of r r with r is equivalent to 1, or

$$P\,P\,r\,r\,r = 1.$$

We can equally well say that the product of u with u is equivalent to 'doing nothing', so we shall have the formula

$$P\,u\,u = 1.$$

Equally the product of r with the product of u by r is equivalent to doing u. So this means that

$$P\,r\,P\,u\,r = u.$$

Here we have enough *information* of a particular kind by means of which we could reach all the rest of the information given in our six by six table.

General rules

It will not be possible to extract this information without some *rules for such extraction.* For example, we have a product of products here, so how can we extract other products from a product of products?

We could introduce a rule that the product of 1 with anything else, is replaceable by this other thing which we already have. In order to express this accurately we need some symbol for this phrase 'something we already have', in other words, for a *general element.* So let us take a similar point of view as the one we took with our arithmetical problem and use frames such as squares, triangles, etc., for an *arbitrary element* constructed out of previously given elements. So our new assumption will look like this:

$$P\;1, \square\; = \;\square \text{ also } P \;\square, 1\; = \;\square$$

The reader may, no doubt, remember that we already had such a general property that described our arithmetical game. This is the first resemblance between the *arithmetical game* and the *triangle game.* It is also fairly obvious that the whole six by six table is *associative.* If the reader has any doubts, he is invited to work it out by trying all the possible sets of three elements, although this would be extremely tedious to do. So we could postulate the associative property for operators in this game, in the same way as we did in the arithmetical game. This will be our second link, our second between the arithmetical game and the triangle game. So we can write

$$P\;P\,\square, \triangle, \square\; = \;P\,\square, P\triangle, \square.$$

The product of the product of the $\square$ by the $\triangle$ with the $\square$ can be replaced by the product of the $\square$ with the product of the $\triangle$ by the $\square$

Axioms, proofs and theorems

The element v can formally be defined as P r, u, the element w as P u r and the element s as P r r. We are then able to express the entire six by six table in terms of r's and u's. For example, we might pick any one part of the table and see if our rules of procedure will now allow us to proceed from the product indicated, that is, from the operators combined, to the product shown in the table. Our contention is that our three pieces of information namely that

$$P\,P\,r\,r\,r = 1,\; P\,u\,u = 1,\; P\,r\,P\,u\,r = u$$

together with the two rules of procedure governing the use of P, will allow us to *demonstrate* that every other part of the table follows from these three pieces of special information. We can do this just in the same way as we did it in the case of arithmetic. Certain arithmetical properties not postulated in the description could be *proved* by the use of the rules of procedure given in that procedural game. Let us take, for example, the statement in the table that

$$P \, w \, u = s.$$

We know, of course, that w is short for P u r and that s is short for P r r. So P w u = s for us means P P u r u = P r r. So this is what we have to *show,* follows from the information already given.

We start with

$$P \, P \, u \, r \, u.$$

We can put a P 1 in front according to the rule that we have just been talking about, so we obtain

$$P \, 1 \, P \, P \, u \, r \, u.$$

Now we know that the 1 can be replaced by

$$P \, P \, r \, r$$

so we have the formula

$$P \, P \, P \, r \, r \, P \, P \, u \, r \, u.$$

Now if we examine the associative law, the way it is expressed, we can see that the second P can be interchanged for the first formula that comes after the second P. This is denoted by a $\square$ in the formula. Now if for the $\square$ we read P r r, then we shall see that we can transform the above formula into

$$P \, P \, r \, r \, P \, r \, P \, P \, u \, r \, u,$$

Now in this formula there is the last sub-formula which runs

$$P \, r \, P \, P \, u \, r \, u.$$

In this we can use the associative principle again by regarding the P u r in it as, say, a 'formula x' which will transform the P r P x u into P P r x u and consequently into P P r P u r u the P u r being the x and so the whole formula will transform into

$$P \, P \, r \, r \, P \, P \, r \, P \, u \, r \, u.$$

But from one of our particular pieces of information we know that P r P u r can be replaced by u and, therefore, the whole formula becomes

$$P \, P \, r \, r \, P \, u \, u.$$

But, again, you know that the P u u can be replaced by 1, so we have

$$P \, P \, r \, r \, 1.$$

Now putting P r r = $\square$, we know that any P $\square$, 1 can be replaced by $\square$, namely here by P r r. So we have transformed P P u r u into P r r by replacing bits of formula by equivalent bits of formula, by means of the rules. We need only add another rule to our formal system to say that we are entitled to put an equal sign between any two formulae in a column of formulae which are obtained from each other by replacing a series of symbols by another series of symbols by which they are allowed to be replaced either in virtue of our general principles or in virtue of our particular rules.

So now we have a formal system with the *particular rules:*

$$P \, P \, r \, r \, r = 1$$
$$P \, u \, u = 1$$
$$P \, r \, P \, u \, r = u$$

and with the *general rules:*

$$P \square, 1 = P\, 1, \square = \square$$

$$P\ P \square, \triangle, \lozenge\ = P\square, P\triangle, \lozenge$$

So by means of these two general rules and the three particular rules, we are able to transform formal series of symbols into *equivalent* series of symbols. This is a *totally abstract and symbolic game.*

The rules of grammar in our abstract game are the rules of transformation. On the other hand the rules of spelling relate to the *ways* in which we write down properties symbolically. It is important to realize what the spelling rules are in our game. For instance, a series of symbols such as P u would not have any meaning because P means 'join something to something else'. And 'join u to' means nothing unless we say to what we wish to join u. P u r has a meaning, but P P u r does not, P P u r u does, because that means that we have to use the function P to join P u r to u. So as long as we observe these rules of spelling in transforming formal sentences into other formal sentences, and as long as we observe the rules of the grammar, we shall be making *valid deductions.* That is, we shall in this way be able to deduce any part of the six by six table from the information given. It is left as an interesting exercise for the reader to pick some other information out of the table and see if he can construct a proof, most meticulously, step by step, to reach this final stage, from his initial stage. This will *prove* that the particular part of the table is *deducible* from the amount of information given, by means of the rules of procedure that we have allowed.

The final stages of learning mathematics

The reader has by now passed through two more stages of learning, if indeed he has followed the previous arguments. The fifth stage consisted in describing the properties of the representations. In the arithmetical case this led us to a certain number of *particular rules,* namely, to the addition facts on which we could build proofs in that system, together with a set of *general rules* which gave us a way to set about transforming a series of operators into other series of operators irrespective of what particular operators they were.

In the case of the triangle game we also have some *particular rules.* The three particular rules previously enumerated are assumed. We also have some *general rules* which correspond very closely to the general rules in the arithmetical game. It will be seen, for example, that the commutativity rule which applied in the arithmetical game no longer applies in this game. P u r is not equal to P r u. In fact, P u r = w and P r u = v.

After a considerable amount of description of our system and development of the language we symbolized what we have learned by means of this language. The symbolization process is a very important part of the learning of mathematics and quite possibly one of the reasons why so few people learn mathematics is because they are forced to this stage too soon and asked to symbolize concepts which they do not understand, that is, for which they have no back-log of any kind of personal experience. The many and varied experiences which we have given in preceeding chapters should have served as background for the reader, if indeed he has carried them out. He should be able to take the leap into the representational and then into the symbolic system after such a playful introduction.

To use symbols is not enough for a mathematician. He needs to put some order into his description as well as some economy. We have selected two particular examples, to illustrate how this process of putting in order can be carried out. In our ordered version in each case we

MATHEMATICS THROUGH THE SENSES

give some particular pieces of information which we class as initial. Then we add certain general kinds of information which form an essential part of the fundamental properties described. Finally, in both cases, we invent a game which we might call the *proof game*. This enables us to reach other parts of the description which are not considered as initial or fundamental. In mathematics the initial descriptions are called *axioms*. The ways of reaching the other descriptions through admitted methods of procedure are known as *proofs*. And the other properties or descriptions so reached are known as *theorems*.

It is a great pity that axioms, proofs, and theorems are bandied about with such ease in most schools without anyone going to the trouble of providing the experiential background which would make such activities meaningful, pleasant and exciting, for both children and adults. It is hoped that this collection of games, followed by attempts to explain the mathematics involved, will make the enjoyment of mathematics just a little more widespread than it is at the time of writing.

Epilogue

DURING THE COURSE of the last few chapters we have been through several different kinds of learning. The initial chapters gave an introduction in the form of fun to certain mathematical ideas to be more clearly structured, later on by further and different kinds of activities.

The very first kind of activity in learning is simply sizing up the situation and experimenting with it. When we come across a new situation we manipulate it in almost a random fashion. When we explore a new town where we have just arrived we walk around in it. We notice a few landmarks. We notice a few interesting spots. We let ourselves go on exploring. We do a similar kind of thing if we are presented with one of these conventional puzzles, 'Instant Insanity' or any other kind of puzzle along these lines. We put things here and there and everywhere just to see what happens. This is the initial exploratory stage which we have called 'free play', and this is the first stage of any kind of learning. We come in contact with the situations in which problems arise, and when we are able to solve a certain class of problems which do arise in these situations by means of a systematic attack on such problem, then we can say that we have learned something in this area.

Now the second stage of learning begins when we have discovered some rules which govern the situation; we have realized that we are able to do certain things and not other things. In fact the manipulation of situations governed by certain rules is the basis of all games. When we play a game we restrict ourselves. We cannot do just anything or it would not be a game. The rules of the game of chess are determined and we have to abide by them or it would not be a game of chess. Any game has the property of restricting us through rules imposed by the game.

Mathematics is full of such restrictions. Certain things are possible and others are not. Now, from the point of view of learning, the mathematical possibilities and impossibilities can be embodied in physical possibilities and impossibilities in certain games that we can set up. The possibilities and impossibilities may be built into the material with which we play so that the mathematically impossible should also be physically impossible and the mathematically possible should also be physically possible. Materials which will do this are known as structured materials. They are beginning to be used in schools and will possibly be used in industry also very shortly. But we can go further and instead of building material out of wood, plastic, or metal which will do certain things and not others, we can invent the rules ourselves and say that certain moves are just not allowed and others are, such as we do in the game of chess or in a game of tennis or in any other kind of game.

When we learn how to manipulate situations during which we restrict ourselves by either physical or self-imposed rules, then we have entered the second stage of learning, the stage of 'structured play'.

Now since mathematics is abstract, it is not really possible to identify mathematics with any one of such games because if we do, the physical properties and the actual physical events we observe and call into existence will be mistaken for mathematical abstractions. So in order to abstract the real kernel of abstraction from the games, we have to play many games which have similar properties in so far as the inner relationships of the moves are concerned. The comparison of one structured game with another structured game, move by move, event by event, and result by result, brings us to a third stage of learning of a mathematical structure. This stage is quite crucial because it is here that we disentangle the abstract from the concrete. We might call this stage the one of abstraction.

Having done such disentangling, we need some means of projecting out of ourselves what we have extracted and made part of ourselves. This is new knowledge, it is our new *abstraction*. To do this projecting we have seen that it is very convenient, and probably very necessary, to make use of what we have called 'representations'. The 'trees', the slide-rules, the arrow diagrams are such representations. Such representations allow us to think in terms of abstract relations and help us to forget about the concrete world from which these abstract relations have been obtained. The states are represented by empty spaces and the ways of getting from state to state are represented by arrows or in any other way in which we wish to represent them. This will allow us to look at the abstraction which we have obtained from the outside, so to speak, as well as verify that we are able to discriminate between one type of concrete situation and another, in so far as one type might be of the form which we have learned and another type might not. This is what we have called 'conceptual discrimination'. If we have learned that a certain type of situation can be represented in some abstract representational form, we must also be able to tell that another type of situation is not so representable, but possibly representable in another representational form. So we have to start looking at the properties of these representations and we have to start comparing one type with another.

This leads us to the fifth stage of learning, that of describing and comparing our representations. These descriptions will, of course, make use of language. In order to make our descriptions as refined as possible we shall need to borrow languages already existing or invent a new language in terms of which we can make the descriptions precise. This stage could be called the stage of 'symbolization'. We learn to use symbols which stand for the kind of abstract events which we have learned to manipulate.

We have seen that after the fifth stage we still need yet another stage, in which we tidy up the situation. During this stage we establish axioms, proofs and theorems, in other words a *formal system*. So we call this last stage of mathematics learning the one of 'formalization'.

Apart from the six successive stages described above, we might consider the roles of the different sense — modalities in learning as possibly forming a system of priorities.

Movement has clearly accompanied learning in the few million years of life on this planet. It is unlikely that we, the human species, are unaffected by this history. Animals, and small children learn to adapt to new situations by bodily movement, thus acquiring skills for acquiring or avoiding objects, for changing the state of affairs in general in which they find themselves. Through this kind of *participatory* activity, organisms eventually internalize whole sets of sequences of behaviour, which are called *concepts*. It would seem sensible to encourage the time-honoured use of the body to form *concepts*. In school, children are required to sit still, fold their arms, look in front and passively receive what is predigested for them. It is small wonder learning is so inefficient.

Movement involves both space and time. The exploration of space, encouraged by special circumstances such as hitting of a ball or sliding on skis, results in SPORT.

The exploration of time results in the observation and producing of RHYTHMS, leading to MUSIC and VERSE.

The combination of the exploration of space and time, i.e. of movement and rhythm, lead to the activity known as DANCE.

Moving about will naturally give rise to *handling objects.* We begin to use our sence of TOUCH, in order to come to grips with details. It is now *beginning* to be admitted in educational circles that TACTILE AIDS to learning are essential for good and reliable results.

Accompanying TOUCH is the sense of SIGHT. We play with colours and shapes when we paint, draw or sculpt, or we do so passively when we enjoy a beautiful cathedral or a breathtaking view.

A great deal of our activities, necessary for survival in our environment, and based on the co-ordination of the sense of movement with those of touch and of sight. It would seem sensible to involve such co-ordination in the planning of learning sequences.

When we begin to reflect on what we have learned, we *talk* about it. This is our fourth sense, that of HEARING, which comes to our aid. It is very useful to

Talk things over

when we are not sure of something. When we want to get on the bottom of a situation we

analyze it.

In any game, there is a certain amount of talking; either we make observations or we debate with each other as to whether the rules have been correctly observed or some such. The usual deathly silence in the schoolroom, reminiscent of children being seen but never heard, testified to our utter disregard of another very important component of learning.

Internalized talking becomes THINKING. We reflect silently instead of aloud. As we have seen, for talking and thinking, we need a language, i.e. a

SYSTEM of SYMBOLS

in terms of which we can carry out our thinking or talking activities. This is the highest level usually reached by most people. To go beyond this stage would involve metaphysical considerations, which are beyond the scope of this book. To sum up, a seemingly sensible *order* in which we might involve our various sense-modalities would be the following

    (1)   Movement   kinesthetic sense.
    (2)   Touch   tactile sense.
    (3)   Sight   visual sense.
    (4)   Hearing   auditory sense.

followed by

SYMBOLIC ACTIVITY known as THINKING.